BLACK ICE

*This book is dedicated
to the Officers, Warrant Officers,
Non-Commissioned Officers & soldiers
of the Household Cavalry*

BLACK
ICE

Corie Mapp

The memoir of a soldier,
double-amputee & world champion

by Corie Mapp & Christopher Joll

NINE ELMS BOOKS

Published in 2021
by Nine Elms Books Ltd
Unit 6B, Clapham North Arts Centre
26–32 Voltaire Road, London SW4 6DH

E *info@nineelmsbooks.co.uk*
W *www.nineelmsbooks.co.uk*

ISBN print 978-1-910533-58-1
ISBN e-book 978-1-910533-59-8

The photographs used are from the author's
collection except where stated.

Cover photograph by Henry Dallal.
Cover and text design, typesetting and layout
by Lyn Davies *www.lyndaviesdesign.com*
Printed and bound in the UK.

CONTENTS

Preface by Les Ferdinand   *vii*

Foreword by the Rt Hon Sir Hugh Robertson   *viii*

A Personal View by Barney Campbell   *x*

PRELUDE A Moment of Truth   *1*

1. Bimshire   *3*

2. Pride and Industry   *19*

3. The Beat of a Distant Drum   *33*

4. A Donkey Walloper in Khaki   *43*

5. A Tin in the Kit   *57*

6. Marilyn Monroe   *68*

7. Mount Doom   *83*

8. Operation MINIMISE   *99*

9. Back on Two Feet   *110*

10. Playing to Win   *122*

11. The Purest Form of Insanity   *132*

12. Life, Death and the Whole Black Thing   *148*

POSTSCRIPT And finally...   *156*

Glossary of Army slang etc   *158*

Index   163

Acknowledgements   173

About the co-author   175

About the Household Cavalry Foundation   177

PREFACE

Les Ferdinand, MBE

Director of Football, Queens Park Rangers Football Club

As a former athlete, I am honoured to write this Preface to Corie's book. In 2015, when I first met Corie at a Help for Heroes charity event, one of the things that struck me the most, when we walked around the golf course and talked about how his injuries had occurred, was that at no stage did he ever show any resentment, bitterness, or apportion any blame to anyone.

From that conversation, I knew that nothing would stop this truly inspiring and unique individual from achieving his goals. No matter what obstacles have come his way in life, he will never give up until he overcomes them.

With sheer determination, strength and courage, Corie has proved to be top of whatever sport he has taken on at an elite level. The incredible list of his personal and professional accomplishments just keeps growing.

I'm now fortunate to call Corie my friend, and marvel at his continued successes. (I'll put aside that he's an Arsenal fan, because he does come to watch the Super Rs!).

I wish Corie all the very best and look forward to seeing his future sporting achievements, hoping that comes in golf.

FOREWORD

Rt Hon Sir Hugh Robertson, KCMG PC DL
Chair, British Olympic Association formerly of The Life Guards

When Corie Mapp's Regiment deployed to the Gulf War, the Commanding Officer of the day signed off the final regimental orders with the phrase: 'Fortune favours the brave'. Reading this extraordinary story, it is striking how Corie Mapp has turned that phrase on its head. By showing great bravery, he has turned around horrific misfortune and set a wonderful example to everyone who reads this beautifully written book.

From start to finish, Corie Mapp's life is a story of triumph over adversity. Leaving school with no qualifications, after service with the Barbados Defence Force Reserves and the Royal Barbados Police Force, neither of which was without incident, he made the journey from Barbados to England. There he joined the British Army's senior Regiment, The Life Guards, which, as part of the Household Cavalry Regiment, has served in every major recent conflict that this country has undertaken. He learned to ride, took part in the intricate ceremonial of The Queen's Birthday Parade, and then served in Afghanistan at the height of the conflict. Alongside colleagues from every sector of society, he faced debilitating heat and a brutal insurgency. Desperately injured, he returned to his Regiment until he was medically discharged, and then pursued a career in elite sport, competing in the Invictus Games in sitting volleyball, and the Para Bobsleigh World Cup and World Championships, while waiting to hear if this sport is to be included in future Winter Paralympic Games. If that were not enough, he has joined the Wiltshire Police during one of the most challenging times for modern policing.

This is a story that should be read in leadership schools and academies around the world. It should also be read by anyone looking for inspiration or wanting to know how strength of character and great positivity can overcome even the most challenging of circumstances. It will tell you much about what is wrong in our society, but also show you how one man, albeit a remarkable one, can set an example and make a difference. Despite the awful events it depicts, it is a story of great hope and achievement in the most testing of circumstances.

Please enjoy the book, but take a few minutes to reflect on the lessons contained in its chapters. Encouragingly, I suspect and hope that this is not the last that we have heard of Corie Mapp.

A PERSONAL VIEW

Barney Campbell
Formerly of The Blues and Royals, author of Rain: A Novel,
and Corie Mapp's Troop Leader in Afghanistan

I remember very clearly a moment I shared with Corie Mapp in the autumn of 2009. We were in a base in the far north-west of Helmand Province called Forward Operating Base (FOB) Edinburgh. A key logistics hub supporting the counter-insurgency efforts in the town of Musa Qala five miles to the east, Edinburgh itself sat in the middle of the desert and was thus relatively secure, compared to many of the other bases we had visited by that point. Our Troop of four armoured vehicles and twelve soldiers had been based in Edinburgh for a week or so, patrolling far into the desert trying to stop the movement of Taliban fighters into Musa Qala. Back in the camp we would help out with sentry duty and, on that particular evening, Corie was in one of the sentry towers as I climbed up the rickety wooden ladder to join him. The sky above us was a mix of red and gold as the sun disappeared behind a dramatic mountain range, far to our west. It was a beautiful sunset.

To set some context, our small group of twelve soldiers had deployed to Helmand Province in the late summer of 2009. By that time the Taliban had been pushed out of the major towns in the province, but in every single one of them – Sangin, Lashkar Gah, Gereshk, Musa Qala – they were pressing on the edges, trying to get back in and to put the populations back under their cruel control. By this point in the conflict, they had honed their Improvised Explosive Device-making (often also referred to as 'roadside bombs') to an art form, and were using them very skilfully to limit our freedom of movement. Casualties had mounted throughout the year in the face of this unseen threat, and movement was often reduced to the pace of a crawling man, as soldiers were unable to trust the very ground they walked on. Back in the United Kingdom the public were becoming ever more aware of the human cost of the operations in Afghanistan, as repatriation processions for the dead were held in Wootton Bassett, and charities such as ABF The Soldiers' Charity and Help for Heroes (H4H) were drawing more attention to those who had been wounded, often exceptionally severely. It was into this environment that 3 Troop, C Squadron, of the Household Cavalry Regiment was sent, along with thousands of others.

We were lucky in our Troop, in that we were extremely tight-knit, with some fantastic characters and a brilliant sense of camaraderie. For me, as the Troop Leader, this was a source of enormous confidence, because I knew that we had not only a happy group, but also one whose moral compass was incredibly strong – every single man could be relied upon to make the right decision in moments of stress. Key in this was Corie. He was a little older than some of the others and had a wealth of life experience behind him. I found this extremely useful and so did the rest of the boys. He possessed a calming and friendly manner that was fantastic in such a dangerous and frightening environment. I felt very lucky to have him in the Troop.

In the sentry tower I can't now remember the exact words that passed between us, but I can recall precisely the feeling that came over me as we talked. I was a little self-conscious that I was in command of some very experienced soldiers, while I was still finding my feet. I didn't mention any of this to Corie in our conversation as we chatted away, but I remember very clearly being reassured by him that our Troop would be all right. It gave me huge confidence and I was enormously grateful to him for giving me that much-needed boost.

What happened to 3 Troop in the course of our tour is not my story to tell here. It is Corie's, and I am so proud of the way in which he has described what happened to us during that hard, exciting, brutal, but rewarding winter, and what happened to him when he was injured. As you will read, when Corie received his injuries, I was not actually there and the operation to evacuate him was led by Troop Corporal of Horse Matthew McGuire. Corie talks more about Matthew in the book, but suffice to say I cannot think of anyone who could have managed things better. I have no doubt whatsoever that a huge factor behind Corie making such a brilliant recovery was the rapidity and bravery with which he was evacuated.

Corie is remarkable. His extraordinary determination to overcome his injuries, and to push the boundaries of his body and mental resilience are examples to all of us. But, even without that, he is still the same man as he was on that evening in the sentry tower at FOB Edinburgh. Calm, measured, humorous and kind, able to see all aspects of an argument and, above all, able to build bridges with people. As a junior officer in a situation that I found very intimidating, and riddled with self-doubt, I remember drawing huge strength not only from that particular conversation but from all of my dealings with Corie. I know he did the same for all the others in 3 Troop. His perspective, and natural concern for others, comes pouring off the pages of this marvellous book, and although he is the last person to ever think of himself, I would like to redress that and raise a toast to this wonderful man: a superb and courageous soldier and sportsman; but beyond that, an exceptional comrade and friend. This is a great story and we are incredibly lucky to have him tell it.

A Moment of Truth

It is late-February 2010 and a soldier is lying in a hospital bed in the Intensive Care Unit (ICU) in the military wing of Selly Oak Hospital (now the Queen Elizabeth Hospital), Birmingham. He is Trooper Corie Mapp, a thirty-one-year-old Barbadian, who is married with three daughters and is serving with the Household Cavalry Regiment, the senior unit of the British Army.

Trooper Mapp is in the ICU because he is very seriously ill, suffering from severe trauma and a life-threatening infection. He has in fact been unconscious since 31st January, when he was blown up by an Improvised Explosive Device (IED) while on active service with his Regiment in Afghanistan.

Without warning, Mapp returns to consciousness. Dimly aware that he is in a hospital bed, and assuming that he must have had an accident, he has only one thing on his mind.

'Nurse,' he calls out to a girl in a military nurse's uniform, hovering by the end of his bed, 'could you take my boots off for me, please? They're really tight and hurting me.'

The nurse has no idea what to say. For not only does Trooper Mapp have no boots on, but since the IED explosion he has no legs either.

Realising that the sudden knowledge that he has been crippled in a life-changing way could deepen Mapp's trauma, she leaves his bedside and seeks out the ICU consultant, who returns with her to the patient. Gently the doctor explains to the Household Cavalryman that his legs have had to be amputated below the knee. In his heavily sedated state, this information does not initially sink in.

'Your family are here to see you,' the doctor adds, with a smile.

A short time later, Corie Mapp sees his wife, Marketha, and his youngest sister, Jackie, enter the ward. Thinking that he is still in Afghanistan, he greets them somewhat unconventionally.

'What the hell are you doing in this shit hole?'

. . .

The story that follows is as told to me in Corie Mapp's own words and those of his wife, Marketha, and of his friend and former comrade-in-arms, Matthew 'Jerry' McGuire. Corie's recollections were often painful for him to remember or to bring back to the surface. I salute him for his honesty and courage.

CHRISTOPHER JOLL

CHAPTER I

Bimshire

Thirty-one years before that moment of truth in Selly Oak, I was born in Bridgetown, Barbados. It was 13th October 1978 and I came into this world in another Queen Elizabeth Hospital, which is kind of a neat coincidence, although needless to say I remember nothing about it. In fact, when I sat down to write this book, I found that an awful lot of my early memories had been blown away with my legs. So recovering my memory has been almost as much of a challenge as standing on my new feet. For that reason, and because in my case the child really is the father of the man, I'm going to start at the beginning.

For those of you who don't know it, Barbados is a small island in the West Indies, just twenty-one miles long and fourteen miles wide. It was colonised by the British in 1625, and under British control it became one of the most important producers of cane sugar in the world. This was an industry that required slave labour, which is how and why my ancestors were brought by force to the island from West Africa. Most of my family remained there after the abolition of the slave trade in 1807, the emancipation of existing slaves after the Slavery Abolition Act of 1833, and independence from Britain in 1966. But from a very young age, I felt that there was more to life than was on offer in Barbados. However, before I could explore the world beyond Bimshire – that's what we locals call Barbados – I had to grow up and get myself an education. First, I need to tell you about my home and my family.

Whatever its history, in my opinion Barbados today is the essence of a tropical paradise. Life on the island is laid back, the people are friendly, we have over two hundred days a year of sunshine, and the beaches are amazing, with some of the best swimming in the world. We also have the purest drinking-water, which is filtered through the limestone on which Barbados rests, and – not surprisingly – the highest quality cane sugar.

I grew up in a little village called Clifton Hall, in the parish of Saint John, on the eastern side of the island. Although it's extremely beautiful, because it's on the Atlantic coast Saint John is not a tourist area. When I was a kid, other Bajans (that's the local name for Barbadians) said that it was backward, because our parish had hardly changed over the years. It was certainly true that it had remained both rustic and very authentic: my mum would buy fish from the fishing boats on the local beaches; other than the rum shops, of which there were plenty, it wasn't very commercialised; there was a terrible bus service and cars were rare, which was just as well because the roads weren't great; and families would still consult the local Obeah woman, who was – amongst many other things – a healer. Barbados is a Christian island, but the old religions and traditions, which our ancestors brought from West Africa, had at that time not entirely disappeared.

People said that we had been neglected by the government, which was certainly true; but even so, most of the families there liked it just the way it was. Best of all, for me, Saint John was (and still is) a family-oriented place and everybody there knew everybody else. It's still somewhere where you would never, ever go hungry, because there is always somebody who would feed you.

Putting all of this together, it's no surprise that Saint John was and is a very quiet part of Barbados. It is also serene. In the early morning, the breeze blows in from the sea through the mile trees, which have long, green tentacles, and as it does so it makes a sort of shush-ing noise. That sound is one of the most calming things that I've ever heard. The countryside around Saint John is quite hilly, a bit like where I live now in

Wiltshire. From the hill behind our house, I could see all the neighbouring parishes: Saint Joseph, Saint George and Saint Philip. Although, as I've said, I have always wanted to explore the world beyond the parish boundary, I've never had any issues with being brought up in Saint John. Our neighbours never changed and our house was surrounded by family. It may have been parochial, but it was *our* parish.

Which brings me to our house. When I was brought home from the hospital, it was to a traditional single-storey Barbados house built from mahogany. I don't remember much about that house, because fairly soon my dad rebuilt it in concrete, although I do remember that I was old enough to help him with the new roof. During the time that work was going on, we lived with my sister Joyce at the nearby village of Edge Cliff, where my cousins, my grandma and my great-grandfather also lived. My sister Sissy's boyfriend and future husband, Errol Mayers, whom we all called Wayne, helped my dad to build the house; he had a dumper truck and brought in the building materials. There's lots more I want to write about him, but that must wait for its proper place.

When our new house was finished it had three bedrooms and a bathroom. My parents had one of the bedrooms, Sissy and Wayne had the second one, and I had my own room. That was one of the perks of being the only boy. The house was cosy, homey, and full of ornaments; being traditional Bajan women, my mum and Sissy took a lot of pride in the way they kept it looking.

Now, having mentioned them without an explanation, I need to tell you about these people, my family.

My dad, Rudolph Mapp, was a qualified carpenter, and I'll come to him in a moment. My mum, Agnes (known as Pinky), who is still with us and whom I've always affectionately called 'Mummy', had been taken out of school by her parents when she was ten and trained as a seamstress – although, by the time I was born, she was a cook in the Barbados school-meal service. I remember her as being very energetic. She used to run something like four miles to get to another village called Massiah Street, or to get a bus to Somerville where she worked. Sometimes my dad would run with her or he would ride a bicycle alongside her. At that time, they would both be up at five in the morning every day; they were very hard-working people. They were also supportive and loving parents.

My mum loved people and, most of all, she loved her kids. That said, she would go the extra mile for anyone and everyone. She's the sort of person who would give you her absolute last, and she raised all of us in that way. She was very loving towards me. In fact, I can't think of a bad moment I've ever had with her, although there were lots of times when I annoyed the hell out of her. When that happened, she would give me a few choice words, and sometimes a slap on the bum. I suppose all kids go through that with their mums.

My dad was a very charismatic man, who took extreme pride in the way he dressed; in fact, he was a proper eccentric dude. He loved music, and he loved to provide for his kids. To do that properly, he had spent a lot of time in Canada before I was born, working on tobacco plantations so as to make enough money for his family.

Ever since he'd married my mum, my dad had wanted a boy, so they had just kept on trying and the result was – at two-yearly intervals – four girls. The eldest is Merleen, who I have always called Joyce and who is twenty years older than me; then there is Marie, known by me as Sissy; she was followed by Monica, who I call Fay; and, finally, there is Jacquline, who I call Jackie and who was fourteen when I arrived.

I think that after Jackie my parents had given up trying for a boy, until my uncle Burkley in London had a son called Andrew. Although Bajan families are not competitive, when my dad heard about Andrew, he said to himself: 'Oh, my God, I want a boy for myself.' So, mum and dad tried again and this time, after a miscarriage, I came along.

My mum had the girls when she was pretty young, but when I arrived she was thirty-nine. The pregnancy was normal until she was full term, when there was a problem: I was facing in the wrong direction and the doctors had to do an emergency C-section. It was that or it would have been bad news for both of us. I spent a couple of days in an incubator, but mum had to spend quite a bit of time recovering from the surgery.

It's important to know that we are a religious family, with a firmly held moral code and a belief in the Christian teaching that 'you reap what you sow'. Two weeks after my birth, I was christened at the Anglican Saint John's Parish Church at Glebe Land. This was the church that I would attend for the next two years with my mum. But from the age of three, I went with my sisters – Jackie and her husband Alvin Haynes, Fay and her husband Frankie Haynes (no relation), and Sissy – to a Pentecostal church, the Abundant Life Assembly in Saint Michael, where they taught Sunday school in the junior church.

The Abundant Life Assembly was friendly and lively – with lots of singing, dancing and praise – and very focused on the family. I went to Sunday school in the junior church, as I couldn't at that age have sat through the long sermons in the main church. During those lessons, I heard stories drawn from the Bible. I loved to hear what God was like and about life in Biblical times, and the teachers painted the most wonderful word pictures. It's a funny thing, but when I went to Afghanistan in 2009, it looked just like the places that I'd heard about in Sunday school. I'm proud to say that my time at the Abundant Life Assembly had a profound effect on the development of my Christian faith and my belief in God; I only stopped going there when I started working. After that, I rather lost touch with the church, but I've never lost touch with my relationship with God.

From an early age, my mum often told me this story: 'I was on my way to work one day. As I was walking, I was saying a prayer, asking God to give me a son – even just for one day. And then He gave me you. And so, I'm going to repay Him, by giving you back to Him.' Those were her words. What she meant, as she later explained, was that she wanted me to serve, just like she did. She served our community, she served in the Mothers' Union, she served in the choir. I got my faith from the church, but I got my appetite for helping people and for service from my mum. I recently found this quote by the legendary boxer, Muhammad Ali, which speaks for us both: 'service to others is the rent you pay for your room here on earth'. Spot on.

Turning back to my dad. When I was born, he had recently given up working in Canada because of his health. He had been diagnosed with arrhythmia and was told not to rush around so much, so he took a job in Barbados doing maintenance work on the estate of a gentleman called Sir David Seale, who owned a rum distillery and a big merchandising business. Sir David was also the top racehorse owner on the island.

My dad loved the job and had a great relationship with his boss; but he worked very long hours, so I didn't see much of him when I was a little kid. However, sometimes he would take me to Sir David's stables, where he introduced me to *Sanford Prince*, who is still the only horse to have won the Barbados Gold Cup three times. I would get to stroke his soft nose and other stuff; I loved it.

On Good Fridays, my dad would take me over the hill at Saint John to fly a big kite that we owned. As well as being an important religious festival, Easter is a kite-flying holiday for kids all over the island. We'd fly our kite all day, until my eyes were swollen from looking up. Not only was it great fun, but we would talk. That's when I really learned about my dad and the way he was, which was a loving and thoughtful person who wanted nothing more than to do the best he could for all of us. That fact, in the light of what happened later, is an important point to remember.

Unfortunately, when I was nine years old, my dad had his first stroke. He was only fifty. His health went slowly downhill from there and he had to take strong medications, including blood-thinners. Over the next few years, although he went back to work, he had a heart attack and several more strokes. As a result, we lost the next step in the development of a father-son relationship.

But before any of that happened, with my dad and my mum working every hour of the day, they didn't have a lot of time to spare for me.

However, I wasn't neglected. In fact, I was a very happy child, who never lacked for anything; and my childhood was really great, although as you will read it had its difficult moments. I loved having stories read to me: my favourite was *Jack and the Beanstalk*. I used to take beans and plant them in the garden, hoping that I could grow a beanstalk that would take me up to the clouds. I know that sounds pretty corny now, but that's what I was like as a kid: a normal, mischievous child, who loved climbing and would get on top of wardrobes and then couldn't get down; I would wash people's clothes in the toilet; and I was fascinated by my mum's iron. I even tried to iron my dad's shirt. That didn't end well: I burned a hole in it *and* the bed underneath. I was also very curious.

I must have been about three when, one Sunday afternoon in the garden, I asked my dad where babies came from. At that moment, there was an aeroplane flying overhead: 'Air Canada drops them out as they fly over – I caught one, and that's how you came along'. I have no idea what made him make up the story. At first, I wasn't convinced but he repeated it, so I reckoned that it must be true. Needless to say, this story became a running joke in the family for years, but it didn't stop me loving aeroplanes and wanting to be a pilot.

For some reason, I also loved boats and buses. Sometimes, I would wander away from home without anyone knowing and go down to the end of the road. There I would sit on the step of Mr Bailey's rum shop and wait for the buses to go past. Then one day, one of our neighbours caught me wandering down there: 'Oh, Corie,' she said, 'where are you going?' I said that I was going to watch the buses. 'You shouldn't be here; I'm taking you home.' Then she led me back to my mum.

That sort of neighbourly behaviour is very typical of Barbados, particularly in our village where everybody looks out for each other. But it also meant that I could never do anything wrong, because someone would know my mum, my dad, or somebody connected to my family. On one occasion, some friends of mine and I were rough-housing around on the road coming home from school, and a lady came out of the cane ground and wanted to know why we were behaving badly. She grabbed me by the arm, spanked my bottom, walked us a little way along the road, and then told me to go home. Later, she told my mum what she'd done, and I got spanked again.

But it wasn't just the neighbours who were strict. My grandfather, who worked for the Ministry of Transport, had a cart drawn by a donkey called *Prince*. I loved them both. On Fridays after work, my grandpa would drive his cart to the nearest rum shop, where he would get completely shit-faced. Fortunately, *Prince*, who was a real character, knew the way home and would take grandpa back to his house when the rum shop closed. Once there, my grandma would help grandpa in, then unhitch *Prince*, who would take himself off to graze knowing that his job for the evening was done. However, when I was with grandpa, he wouldn't let me get away with anything. My sisters were the same, which brings me to Sissy, who is the most loving person that you could ever conceive, a real saint; she became like a second mother to me. A lot of people actually thought that she *was* my mum.

At this time, Sissy was a Troop Leader in the Brownies and when she went away to Brownie camp, I would get sick. It was so bad that I would vomit and get seriously depressed. In fact, I just couldn't cope, such was the relationship that I had with her. She and Wayne, whom she married in 1985, guarded and protected me, and it was Sissy who took me every day to my first school, Hothersal Primary, where I started at the age of three. She could do this because she was unemployed; my other older sisters were working and Jackie was still too young.

As I've said, I was a very happy child – but I did *not* like my time at Hothersal Primary, which was run on 'English lines'. I think that the main reason I didn't like it was that I was left-handed; and in those days, you had to write with your right hand. If I was caught writing with my left, I would be beaten and then told to 'go to the pigsty', which meant sitting under my desk. There was also a school bully who picked on me, until my maternal grandma, Claudine Young, who collected me for lunch every day, sorted him out after I'd told her. 'Show me which kid is giving you trouble,' she said, when we went back after lunch. I pointed out the boy in the play-ground and she marched me over to him. She wasn't a violent woman, but she was very protective of me. 'Punch him in the stomach,' she ordered me. I hesitated, so she repeated the order and I obeyed. As the bully and I were both finding out, you didn't mess with grandma Young. 'If you ever touch my grandson again,' she told the boy, 'that's what will happen to you.' This was rough justice, but he never bothered me again.

Talking of grandma Young, she had a huge personality and there are tons of family stories about her, for which there is no space here, except for this one. Years earlier, before I was born, a girl at school had hit one of my sisters. Grandma Young told my sister: 'Go and sort it out and don't come back until the job is finished'. She did as grandma ordered, the kid then complained to her parents, who in turn complained to my grandma. 'That was very wrong of her,' she said, pushing my sister inside the house, 'leave it to me.' Once in the front house – that's what we call the front room – she picked up a large cushion and a carpet beater. 'Every time I hit the ottoman, scream as loud as you can,' grandma said. A few minutes later the girl's complaining parents went away pacified.

My problems in the school room were less easily solved, and as I've said, I really hated Hothersal. The head had her favourites and I was definitely not one of them. My unhappiness there was also not helped by a terrible tragedy that happened in our village, when a house caught fire and burned down. Inside the burning house was a girl who I used to play with. I saw her being carried away on a stretcher, screaming; she had been very badly burned and later died in hospital. This awful event really upset me and was definitely the most traumatic event of my childhood. Perhaps not surpris-ingly, I started to have the same sickness as when Sissy went to Brownie camp. The tragedy was national news and the Prime Minister, Errol Walton Barrow, came to visit our village. He was a local man who knew my parents, and hearing that I was very upset, he spoke to me. Afterwards, he told my mum that even though I was only four, I had a very good sense of self, a good way with words, and that someday my words would 'take me places'. I hope that this book shows he was right.

A few months after that awful fire, Sissy announced she was going to England for the summer holidays, to stay with my uncle Fitz Young in Derby. Needless to say, I got sick again at this news. That Sunday I was in church and the pastor asked if anybody had any needs. Nobody said anything, so I slipped away from my sisters and went up to the pastor at the altar. 'I want to go to England with Sissy,' I told him, 'but I haven't got the money.' 'If you pray hard enough, Corie,' he replied, 'you will go.' Well, I had a lot of faith as a little boy (and still do), so I prayed and prayed – and I got the money for my trip. Some of it was contributed, so I heard later, by Prime Minister Barrow.

The trip to England that summer was a life-changer for me. One weekend we went down to London to see the sights, including Buckingham Palace. When I saw the Foot Guards and watched the Changing of the Guard, I just fell in love with the whole thing. I told Sissy that I wanted to live that dream and afterwards I could think of little else. Sadly, the holiday was soon over and we flew back to Barbados. But once we were home, every time I saw a British Airways advert, which in those days always featured Buckingham Palace and the Guards, it reinforced my ambition to be a part of it.

Back once more in Barbados, one of the janitors at Hothersal Primary, a lady called Miss Gibson, told my mum what had been happening to me in school and that I wasn't really learning anything. 'He needs to be moved to a different school,' she said. So although my dad's health was getting worse, I was moved to Codrington High School, a very posh place with both white and black pupils. I was five years old and it was my first encounter with white people.

But before I tell you about Codrington High, I need to focus for a moment on the second most important father figure in my life after my dad: Sissy's husband, Wayne, who helped build our new house and then lived with us there. Wayne never said anything about it, but I guess that he realised my dad was struggling to do some of the things that dads are supposed to do with their sons, and he quietly filled in some of those gaps. He'd organise picnics and barbecues for the family. On Sunday evenings, in the front house, my dad would turn off the TV, sit in his chair tapping his foot, and watch Sissy and Wayne dancing like crazy people to the Drifters, Brook Benton, and all that 1950s and '60s stuff. Sometimes, Wayne would organise awesome games of Monopoly, in which he was always the banker. I may not have learned much maths at Hothersal, or later at Codrington, but those games of Monopoly certainly taught me how to count – and how to hold my own.

As well as the contracting work that he did with his dumper truck, Wayne had pigs and cows, and kept more than a hundred chickens behind our house. As often as I could, I worked with him, and every day after school, I would go with him to feed the pigs or help him move the cows to another field. Wayne also managed the Saint John's Cultural Cricket Club at Gall Hill, which is where I learned to play, and with his encouragement became quite a good bowler. I was good enough, so Wayne thought, to try out for the school team. I did and got a place, but for some reason I've now forgotten, I never played for that team. At other times we'd sit amongst the guava trees behind the vicarage, where he sometimes grazed the cows, looking out to sea, and he'd talk to me about life and becoming a man. It was Wayne who helped me with the lost parts of my boyhood, and it was he who helped me to survive Codrington High, which is where I was sent just before my sixth birthday.

Looking back, my time at Codrington is a bit of a blur. I certainly didn't learn much there, and although I was keen to integrate, it wasn't helpful that the school sports revolved around tennis, when I was only interested in cricket, gymnastics and football. It also wasn't great that my mum had told the school not to 'spare the rod' where I was concerned, which led to me frequently being spanked in front of the whole class. I tried my best to be liked and to fit in, but it wasn't long before I sort of shut down, stopped trying, and retreated into my shell.

My time at Codrington, where I was a pupil for three years, wasn't helped by the arrival from New York of my cousin Michelle, the daughter of my uncle Herbert Young. He wanted her to get a British-style education, which is what Codrington High specialised in, believing it to be better than the one on offer in the States. So she came to live with us and I got saddled with her. Every morning she joined me on the trip to school. It was at least a mile-and-a-half from our house to the bus stop and Michelle, who was rather slow, often made me miss the bus; as a result, I would arrive late at Codrington, which got me into trouble with my teacher. It was the same going home. I think Michelle may have told the other girls at school that I was being hard on her over this, and one day they all ganged up on me, which certainly didn't help me to like Michelle.

Even without the problems caused by my cousin, I was having a tough time at Codrington until a British teacher called Susan Warrington took me under her wing. She had realised that I learned quickly from the spoken word, but that I really struggled learning from books. When I read, I don't 'get it' in the same way as when I listen. My wife Marketha says that when she reads it's like a story unfolding in her head; but with me that doesn't happen. This was something that the other teachers didn't understand about me, with the result that I was learning practically nothing. In fact, I struggled with everything. That situation might have gone on indefinitely had another teacher not told my mum, who came to the school to see for herself what was or wasn't going on. I wasn't expecting her, and without me knowing she watched me just looking around the class, not doing much and certainly not engaging with the lesson.

Thinking about it now, my mum and dad should never have sent me to Codrington High. I was a local kid and most of my friends went to the local schools. But my parents wanted me to have what they thought was the best education available, and so they worked their arses off to pay for my time at Codrington. I stood out from the crowd; their families were better off than mine and they all knew each other. The result was that I became even more of a loner and this led to fights, sometimes with a white boy called Paul Cave. These fights weren't racial, we just didn't like each other. God only knows what would have happened had I stayed at that school.

Fortunately, at the time my mum was working at Mount Tabor Primary. This was a state school and nothing like as 'smart' as Codrington High. Realising after her visit that I wasn't getting an education where I was, she moved me there. When I arrived at Mount Tabor, yet again I rather stood out from the crowd. This time it was because, after Codrington High, I didn't speak or behave like the other kids. Sometimes you can't win! Nonetheless, I wanted to fit in, and in one way Codrington High helped me to do this. Although I hadn't learned stuff like mathematics and English grammar there, I had absorbed a lot of general knowledge. At Mount Tabor there was a school quiz team, and those facts that I had learned at Codrington got me onto it pretty quickly. My eventual acceptance was also helped by the fact that games at Mount Tabor were cricket and athletics, not tennis, and it wasn't long before I was also representing the school in those sports. So, it was quizzes and games that helped me to make friends there.

Back in the Mount Tabor class room, and thanks to my teacher, Miss Wiltshire, I was actually starting to learn, which was just as well, as I was very behind in my studies and not far off having to sit my Common Entrance, the Barbados equivalent of Eleven-Plus. Miss Wiltshire spent a lot of time rebuilding my confidence, aided by the support of Mr Batson, the headmaster, who was a strict but very caring man, and my maths teacher, Mr Burke, who at last got me to understand long division and multiplication. He was a legend. I also got extra coaching in English from Miss Stewart, a teacher who lived in the nearby village of Venture.

After three years at Mount Tabor, I had just about caught up and could deal pretty well with the verbal tests that were set by Mr Batson. He would come into our class room without warning and say, for example: 'Mr Mapp, what's the plural of sheep?' He did this not only to test our knowledge, but also to test our confidence ahead of sitting Common Entrance. If you got the answer wrong, you got lashes. More rough justice, but it worked and I was pretty confident about passing Common Entrance, until I had an accident at school.

I will spare you the details, but one day, shortly before the exam, I was rough-housing in the class room and smashed my groin onto the edge of a desk. It hurt like hell, but I didn't want to tell anyone. That night I was in real pain – sweating, crying and so on – and eventually I couldn't stand it anymore and showed my swollen nuts to my mum. The next thing that I knew I was in hospital, and the following day I was operated on. That solved the problem, but I didn't get back to school for nearly two weeks, and that meant that I lost some valuable revision time. Nonetheless, I passed the exam in May 1990, although not perhaps as well as I might have done.

Before you take Common Entrance in Barbados, you have to list your preferences for secondary school in descending order; the choice of which you go to depends on your grades. I wanted to go with my mates at Mount Tabor to The Lodge School, or another local one (there was plenty of choice). But for some reason my mum put the Garrison Secondary School on my list – and with my grades, that was where I was sent.

Garrison Secondary was a town school, on the other side of the island in Dalkeith, a southern part of the capital, Bridgetown. Mostly town boys went there, and consequently it was pretty rough. I was a country kid with no experience of gangs or gang violence, and frankly my first days at the Garrison scared the shit out of me. I'd been there less than a week, when I was robbed in the playground by some Fifth Formers. Grandma Young had taught me to fight back, and so later in the day I retaliated. The result was that I ended up in the Principal's office where I was offered the choice of suspension, or to take some lashes and join the Barbados Cadets Corps.

It's funny now to think that the Cadets was a punishment, because it was the making of me. This was thanks largely to Captain Ralston Nichols, the Officer Commanding the school's No 14 Cadet Company. He would become the third most influential father figure in my life, after my dad and Wayne. Once I'd left the Principal's study, rubbing my bum, Captain Nichols spoke to my mum: 'I know he's sound, give him to me and I'll make him a man.' So she did, and it wasn't long before I'd fallen in love with the Cadets Corps.

Every Tuesday and Friday after school, under Captain Nichols' direction, we learned drill, map-reading, field craft, and conflict resolution. And there was a bonus, because in the Cadets' hut there were lots of pamphlets about the British Army, with photos of the Guards. 'Yes,' I said to myself, 'at last I'm in a place from where I can follow my dream'. Better still, I made lots of real friends, and that in turn helped me to fall in love with the school that I initially hated. I hung out with other Cadets and we got up to all kinds of mischief, the details of most of which I have forgotten.

I also made some good friends through cricket, including Tino Best and Dwayne Smith, both of whom went on to play for the West Indies. I do remember one adventure with Tino, because we ended up on TV. We were at the old Kensington Oval, Bridgetown's main cricket ground, watching Pakistan play the West Indies. For some reason, perhaps to get a better view, we talked our way through a number of the stands and managed to climb up onto the clock tower, above the players' pavilion, where we were spotted by a television cameraman – and the whole of Barbados.

Back in the class room, I was about average academically and I really liked science, which I would need if I was to fulfil my then ambition to be a pilot. I hadn't forgotten about the Guards, and at that time I hoped to be able to combine the two dreams. Anyway, at the end of Third Form I had to choose my subjects for the CXC Exams, the Barbados equivalent of GCSE, and when I told my teacher that I wanted to take those subjects that would help me to get my pilot's licence, she was very dismissive. 'Forget it,' she said, 'your mother could never afford to pay for the training. You should do art.'

So I joined the art class, stopped working, and concentrated on athletics and the Cadets. Whenever I could, I would skip class. Nonetheless, I sat the exam, and so the school said, did very well. But there was a problem: my course work had been mislaid, so I couldn't be given a grade. The school then tried to make me stay on and do the exam again, even promising me that I would get promoted in the Cadets to sergeant major. I was tempted, then I thought to myself: 'If the only reason I want to stay in school is because I will be a big boy in the Cadets, what's the sense of that?' It was a question that had one simple answer. I spoke to my mum about it, she spoke to the Barbados Youth Service (BYS), and I left the Garrison Secondary School in July 1995 without any qualifications, but ready to start the next chapter of my life.

CHAPTER 2

Pride and Industry

I JOINED THE BARBADOS Youth Service in September 1995 and spent the next twelve months on their development programme. The BYS had been established in 1991 by the government of Barbados to provide life skills training for young Bajans, and to give them some direction. My mum thought that the course might help me to get some perspective on myself, and so I enrolled and reported to Queen's Park Steel Shed in Bridgetown to start the course. I was one of about thirty other people, ranging in age from late-teens to early-twenties, some of whom I knew from my 'year' at school. We were put into groups and allocated a councillor: mine was Mr Joseph Riley, who came from the parish of Saint Joseph, which is next door to Saint John.

It was immediately clear to me that Mr Riley was tough, straight-talking, and a strict disciplinarian – but he was also fair. Over the course of the next few days, I came to respect him enormously, and as a major influence on my future life, I am proud to say that he became a bit of a father figure to me. I have been lucky that at critical points in my life there have always been good people who have stepped in and pointed me in the right direction. Mr Riley was one of those people.

Although we were a mixed group and our number included some pretty rough types, who were victims of their upbringing, the course itself was really enjoyable. It gave me some much-needed self-discipline and on it I made several life-long friends. Every day we would undertake tasks that included drill (we were good enough at that to be included on the Independence Day Parade), drama, and even basic seamanship (which led to my gaining my speedboat licence). Every Friday we would meet with Mr Riley to review our progress, and twice during the year we went away to a residential camp for two weeks.

This was at Harrison Point, Saint Lucy, Barbados's northernmost parish. Designed to be a 'boot camp', which the dictionary defines as being 'an immersive experience during which participants enhance their careers by learning new skills', we were totally cut off from our families and the outside world. The core activity at Harrison Point was survival training. It was tough, but I took away from those camps both mutual respect for my colleagues and an understanding of the very real benefits of team work. Even though we started out as a mixed bunch from widely different backgrounds, including quite a few Rastafarians, by the end of that year we were one family and each of us had discovered what we were good at.

In my case, I realised that I was good at art and should develop those art skills that I had gained (and neglected) in school. Yes, I was good at drill, had fallen in love with the Guards, excelled in the Cadets and still wanted a pilot's licence; but at that moment I didn't consider that my next step would be to join the military. In any event, that was not what my father wanted me to do. So instead, I joined a company called Indi Marketing as a trainee. There I was mentored by a great guy called Hudson Griffith, who made it his objective to help me into art and printing. In some ways he was too successful. Although I was offered a long-term job with the company, which even undertook to pay for further skills training, it wasn't long before I decided that I needed to go back to school and get a printing qualification.

In September 1996, I enrolled on a two-year graphic arts and printing course at Samuel Jackman Prescod Polytechnic (since 2017, the Samuel Jackman Prescod Institute of Technology), based at Pinelands in Saint Michael parish, south of Bridgetown. While I was there, I studied English, maths and printing. More importantly, I was studying alongside my old friend, Tino Best. I also met Renier Grace, with whom I developed a deep friendship and who will appear often in these pages; and I acquired my first girlfriend, along with a love of volleyball. In fact, I became so good at volleyball, that coached first by Peter Went and then by the awesome John Stuart, I played for the Combined Schools team and was even considered (but not chosen) to play for the Junior National team.

Despite these distractions, I now really enjoyed the business of learning. In 1998 I graduated from the polytechnic with a Diploma in Photo Offset Lithography & Printing, and almost immediately got a job with a company called COT Printery. That lasted until I was fired, four months later. Rather crushed by this setback, I bummed around at home until my mum arranged for me to be apprenticed to the Barbados Government Printing Department. There I earned a miserable 100 Barbados Dollars a week (2021: £35.00), which was barely enough to pay my bus fare to-and-from work and buy lunch. I didn't need to be told that this was just existing.

So when an old friend from the Cadets called Andre Jordan told me that the Barbados Defence Force (BDF) was organising a Cadet Reserve training camp and asked if I was interested, I jumped at the idea. Soon after this I was contacted by Captain Ingus Begg of the BDF, who arranged for me to join Bravo Company, the 'tip of the spear' of the Barbados Regiment, which is the Reserves Battalion of the BDF.

This was a paid appointment that involved training on Thursday nights; public duties on official occasions, such as the Remembrance Day and Independence Day Parades held on the Garrison Savannah Racecourse in Bridgetown; and night-time patrols with the Royal Barbados Police Force (RBPF). These last included 'cane-fire patrols', to prevent arson in the sugar cane fields; 'gully patrols', to disrupt the criminal gangs using the extensive watercourses that criss-cross Barbados as safe hides for illegal drugs; and 'drugs ops', to intercept drug-runners landing their stuff along the island's extensive coast line. If I had to be a printer by day for a pittance, I now had the real reward of serving my country by night. But printing and soldiering were not my only commitment at that time, for in 1999 I also became a Parish Ambassador.

The Parish Ambassador scheme had been established three years previously by the Barbados government, and was designed to engage young people in the improvement of their local communities and thereby in the nation as a whole. Appointment to the role was by a local competition, and the assignment lasted for twelve months. During that year, the Parish Ambassadors (one of each sex for each parish) would propose and then execute a community project, ending the year with a national pageant and project presentation, about which more in a moment.

Wayne encouraged me to put my name forward, which I did in partnership with a friend called Lisa Haynes (now Lisa Brome). This led to a meeting at which, in competition with several others, we were asked to describe our project. Lisa and I had given this a lot of thought and our proposal was to unite the parish using cultural projects. We needed, we said, to get back to our roots by promoting Saint John traditions, particularly local food, that had been pushed aside by the creeping Americanisation of the island. We also proposed to recognise the good people in our parish and feature several Saint John parishioners as role models, including the late Prime Minister, Errol Walton Barrow, and Graydon Sealy, the headmaster of the Garrison Secondary School (since renamed in his honour). The result was that we were appointed to the role.

Over the course of the next twelve months, Lisa and I were kept busy hunting down lost recipes, organising local cultural events and touring other parishes. During this time I met Marketha, who was one of the Parish Ambassadors for Saint Philip. I also got to take Mr Sealy on an aerial tour of the island. Despite the disparaging remark made by the teacher at my secondary school about my mum's ability to pay, she had put up the money for me to start pilot training.

With my day job, my engagement with the Reserves and the ambassadorial role, 1999 flew by. Almost before I knew it, I found myself with Lisa on the stage at the end-of-year pageant. In front of a large crowd and TV cameras, we presented our project as the middle section of a three-part competition, involving a parade of themed costumes (ours were based on the Saint John parish church and its famous sundial), and a parade of formal costumes. As each parish has a colour (Saint John is gold because, as the easternmost parish, we first see the rising sun, and Marketha's parish colour is purple), the whole event is very vibrant.

Lisa and I had high hopes of winning this competition. For a start, our costumes were streets ahead of the other parishes' efforts. By the time we got to make our presentation on stage, we were confident that we were in the lead. However, when it came to my turn to speak, despite having gathered lots of experience of public-speaking during the year, I panicked and completely 'dried'. In front of thousands of spectators and live on national television, I couldn't remember a damned thing that I had rehearsed. As the crowd grew restive and some even started to heckle, Lisa rushed to my rescue, and somehow we managed to make it through to the end. The result of my performance (or lack of it) on stage was that instead of winning, and despite a really good parade of our formal wear, we came second. I was devastated that I had let down both a colleague and my community. In my disgust at myself, I passed the prize of a trip to St Lucia to my volleyball team.

At about this time my dad started talking to me about the police. Part of the reason for this was that, knowing of my dream to be in the Guards, he really didn't want me to take my military activities any further, particularly if they might involve me leaving Barbados. In addition, his health wasn't improving and as his only son, the responsibility for his family would fall on me if he died. So I think he wanted to see me secure in a respected and decently paid job before that happened.

With plenty of friends and some relations in the RBPF, and knowing that my dad's health was deteriorating, I didn't resist this proposal and applied to be a special constable. In due course, I sat and passed the entry exam and successfully negotiated the interviews, first with a sergeant at RBPF HQ, then with the District C (southern station) station sergeant, and finally with the Commissioner of Police himself. Not long after this, I got a letter informing me that I had been accepted for training, and given a date on which to report to Station Sergeant Maycock, the lady who ran the HQ stores, to draw my uniform, prior to starting the six-week training course.

On the appointed day, Sissy came with me to Bridgetown, and while she waited outside, I reported to Station Sergeant Maycock. 'Name?' she demanded. 'Corie Mapp. I'm here to draw my uniform.' She looked down her list and her forehead creased in a frown. 'What did you say your name was?' 'Corie Mapp,' I replied. 'And which branch have you been assigned to?' 'Special Constable,' I said, firmly. She looked through her papers again. 'Well, you're not on my list. Are you sure you got the letter?' she asked. 'Yes – but I've left it at home,' I replied, rather weakly. 'Hmm… wait a minute.' She picked up another list and starting looking through it, while I wondered what the hell was going on. 'Found you,' she said with a smile. 'The bad news is that you are *not* going to be a Special Constable…' my stomach dropped '… but the good news is that you are going to be a full Constable.' 'What does that mean?' I asked, in disbelief. 'It means, Mr Mapp, that I am to issue you with a constable's uniform and your number – which is 1495 – and you will then go over to the PT Centre to draw your white PT kit. You will report back here tomorrow morning to take the transport to the Regional Police Training Centre (RPTC) for the start of the six-month residential course.'

I staggered out, hardly believing what I had heard. When I told Sissy what had happened, she gave me a big hug. As a full constable, my salary would be far more than I was then earning from the Barbados Government Printing Department and the Reserves, which would enable me to give financial support to my family. That far outweighed having to give up the Barbados Regiment and printing. The rest of the day passed in a bit of a blur and the following morning, after Sissy had helped me pack, I was back in Bridgetown waiting for the bus that was to take us to the RPTC, near to Grantley Adams Airport in Christ Church parish, on the south coast of Barbados. On arrival there, I found that I was part of a large course of fifty-seven police trainees. Many of them came from other eastern Caribbean islands, as the RPTC is – as its name implies – not just a training centre for Bajan policemen.

The six months of that training course were some of the best days of my life. We were housed in dormitories, in a jumble of backgrounds, ages and nationalities. Our instructors were impressive, and some were outstanding: I particularly remember Christine Stanford, who was ex-BDF, very sharp, super-strict, and a drill star; I also remember with considerable respect, Sergeant Graham, another disciplinarian but friendly with it. I did well on the course, except for swimming, which (like many black people) I have never fully mastered. I thoroughly enjoyed our training, which covered the law, firearms, civil unrest, and community policing, which is now of considerable use to me. Although the course was residential, if we passed the weekly exams, we were allowed home at weekends. Those who didn't get home would be assigned to block-cleaning tasks or other admin duties. On the rare occasions when I didn't get a weekend leave pass, I was still happy because I could spend hours watching the civil aeroplanes taking off and landing at the airport.

I should add here that during the course we were 'charged' or fined five Barbados Dollars for minor disciplinary infringements. I incurred many such charges for staring at aeroplanes flying overhead, particularly when we were on the drill square. This became a running joke with the instructors and the other students. The instructor who fined me most often was Station Sergeant Dale Stephens, a big burly man with a massive moustache, a fantastic sense of humour, and a nose for finding our contraband in the dormitory. I can't now remember how many times he yelled at me: 'Mapp - you're charged!'

In July 2001, we reached the end of the course and the Pass Out Parade, which mum, dad, Sissy and Marketha all attended. I had got myself into the final of the drill competition, but I came last. This time I wasn't upset, as I recognised that the others were simply better than me. Any disappointment that I did feel was blown away when I saw the look of pride on my dad's face. I'm sure he knew that he only had a few more years to live; but - at last - he had seen me make something of my life and I had fulfilled his dearest wish for me. That was a result for both of us.

My first posting as a fully-fledged constable was to the Central Police Station in Bridgetown and my first duty was on a night shift. It was a surreal feeling to step out onto the pavement of the capital of my country as a police officer. Probably because of my consistently good turnout and record-keeping, it wasn't long before I came to the attention of Assistant Superintendent 'Fancy Basket' Broome. He would often single me out at Roll Call, always using only my number, and would then look me over or examine my notebook. I always seemed to meet with his approval and never had any problem answering his technical questions, which he would fire without warning, a particular trademark of his. One day he called me into his office, congratulated me yet again, and assigned me to a mobile patrol that night. This was long before I could have expected, in the normal run of events, to be given such a privilege.

Despite the approval of the assistant superintendent, not everything at Central was plain sailing. The only crime target that we were set was to achieve a minimum of twenty-five traffic offence prosecutions every month, which was an easy number to log, particularly in Bridgetown. On one particular shift, the duty sergeant was a man who also happened to own a large number of public service vehicles, including minibuses and taxis. For some reason that I can't now recall, on that particular shift I was in a black mood, and I quite legitimately worked off my temper by issuing 120 traffic violation notices, including failing to stop at a junction, overloading public transport, and so on. One particular recipient of my zeal was a lady who objected strongly to being reported for driving without due care. So angry was she, that she ended up shouting at me: 'Instead of issuing this stuff, you should be chasing murderers.' I asked her if she had anything else to say to me. 'Yes,' she yelled, 'fuck off!'

In the face of this verbal onslaught, I managed to remain cool and polite. However, by the time I got back to the station for my break before the end of my shift, the duty sergeant was in a less than pleasant mood himself. He had been inundated by complaints from, amongst others, the drivers of his vehicle fleet and the irate and foul-mouthed lady. 'I think you've made quite enough waves for one day, youngster,' he said, through gritted teeth and showing a restraint that the lady had not, 'go and chill out on the desk until you have finished your shift.'

When not patrolling the streets of Bridgetown, I would sometimes find myself on the Governor-General's Guard, where more often than not, I would share the duty with Terry Thompson, with whom I'd been in training. The Guard involved six of us reporting to the Governor-General's residence, where we would man the gate and patrol the grounds. It was a very easy duty, with plenty of down time. I had been learning to ride a motorbike, and the police motorcycle patrolmen parked-up at the residence were quite happy for me to practice on one of their machines.

At this time, the Governor-General was Sir Clifford Husbands, an elderly and very benevolent Bajan. One day, he saw me riding around his garden. 'Who taught you to ride?' he asked me, when I pulled up alongside him. I replied that I had taught myself. 'I hope I'm not disturbing you,' I added. 'Not at all,' he said, 'it doesn't bother me in the least.' After that I often saw Sir Clifford walking in the grounds, and he always invited me to join him on a bench, where he quizzed me about my life and policing. He was a proper gentleman, who died in 2017 at the grand old age of ninety-one.

Back at Central, sometime around the middle of 2001, I was once again called into the assistant superintendent's office. '1495,' he said, 'you haven't been here long, but I'm impressed. I'm seconding you to District A where you will join the Rapid Response Unit (RRU) for Operation EAGLE.' This, I knew, was a new initiative to address a sudden rise in violent crime on the island. It seemed that my career was taking off, and as an added bonus, Terry Thompson was being transferred with me.

The RRU was based at District A Station, Station Hill, Bridgetown. Here, the unit was co-located with other police units including the Mounted Section, the Canine Unit, and the Special Services Unit (SSU). At that time, there was some overlap between the RRU and the SSU, particularly in relation to domestic policing. While the RRU was Barbados-centric, the SSU was a response unit for the whole of the eastern Caribbean, and its role included tasks across the islands, such as dealing with serious prison riots or the aftermath of hurricanes. Another difference was that the SSU wore military-style combat kit, while the RRU was dressed either in civvies or a police uniform known as 'red stripe'.

Within Operation EAGLE, a major anti-crime offensive, the RRU's resources were focused on 'hit block' operations, in which we targeted known centres of criminal activity, particularly crimes relating to illegal drugs. We also conducted random 'stop and search' across the island, to intercept (amongst other things) illegal firearms; and – based on intelligence received – intercepted drug landings on the coastline, with which I was already familiar from my time with the Reserves. It was during Operation EAGLE that I cut my active policing teeth, and it gave me some of the best times that I experienced while serving with the RBPF.

After three months, Operation EAGLE ended. However, instead of being returned to Central, the secondment of Terry and me to the RRU was made permanent. For historical reasons, at this time the RRU did not enjoy the same respect as the SSU, and it was decided that this needed to change. The impact on us was that we were often deployed with the SSU, and we got to do just about everything by way of crime policing. In fact, we took serious crime on the island by the scruff of the neck and brought many cases to court. This resulted in my having to spend a lot of my supposedly free time giving evidence there, but I didn't mind.

One case in particular sticks in my mind. We received intelligence that in my own home parish of Saint John, there was a covert marijuana farm operating out of a house next to a gully, from which the 'weed' (marijuana) farmer was able to channel the water needed to grow the illegal plants. When we raided the house, we uncovered the largest marijuana crop that I have ever seen. It took several vans to cart away the drugs, and by the time we returned to the station, we all stank of the stuff.

The high rate of success achieved by the RRU caused tensions with the SSU, and in 2003 the two units were merged. I wasn't altogether happy with this, as the RRU was a real family and that spirit was lost when we amalgamated. I also had a problem with a particular SSU operation, in which I and two other officers, one of whom worked on the police firing ranges, were tasked with breaking-up a cock-fighting ring. I don't want to go into the details, but I was very uncomfortable with the way that the operation was handled. In my view, if the bad lads run off at the approach of the police, then they are showing us respect; if they stay and give us a mouthful, then they need to be taught respect. On this occasion, they ran off. However, one of my colleagues was determined to teach them a lesson. I objected and he accused me of cowardice. This incident was to have consequences for me, as will in due course become apparent.

I've previously mentioned that I met Marketha during my role as a Parish Ambassador. In the months that followed, we grew closer and the relationship progressed from that of friends to lovers. When I became a police constable in 2001, I was able to give her some financial support, as she was then still in full-time education. Later that year, she went through a difficult patch, so I gave her a return airline ticket to England to cheer her up. This enabled her to visit the country for the first time, with my sister Sissy.

The following year, I passed my driving test. One evening I rented a car, took Marketha to a friend's party, and then as I often did slept over at her house. The following morning while still in bed, with the sunlight streaming in through the open window and a light on-shore breeze blowing the curtains around, I raised the question of us getting married. I would like to tell you that I then leapt out of bed, knelt down and did the whole romantic proposal bit. The truth is, that didn't happen. But by the time we sat down to breakfast, we were engaged. This came as a huge relief to my mum, who knew that Marketha was carrying our first child, and had been putting considerable pressure on me to make an honest woman of my girlfriend.

We got married in a simple but beautiful ceremony on 21st December

2002 at Saint John's parish church. My dad and Renier Grace stood jointly as my 'best man'; Marketha's sister Andrea was her maid of honour, and other family members acted as her bridesmaids. I collected Renier on my way to the church. Almost immediately, he asked me if I was 'ready for this'. 'I don't know,' I replied, 'but it feels right.' All went well until we got to the church, where it was immediately obvious that my dad was in a highly emotional state, and that set me off. As the tears ran down my face, Marketha's mum, Ucelia, came up and gave me a hug. 'I'm *very* happy,' I sobbed. At that moment Renier, who is always cool, calm and collected, broke into a huge laugh. That did the trick, the tears stopped, the wedding went ahead without a hitch, and after the reception Marketha and I headed off to a hotel for our honeymoon. Sadly, we hadn't been honeymooning for long before Marketha felt unwell, so we decided to break off the holiday and return home. Three months later, on 18th March 2003, our daughter Erin was born.

Because of the cockfighting incident and other things, soon after Erin was born I applied for a transfer to the Canine Unit. It wasn't long before I was interviewed by a real character called Sergeant McGeary and in mid-2003 made the transfer. On arrival, I was allocated an elderly dog called *Ben* and started my training under a lady called Cerepha 'Tracy' Bridge-man, who had a brilliant dog called *Digby*. Two things quickly became apparent: Tracy was the best in the business and my dog was past his best. I knew about Tracy long before I joined the unit – she was a legend in the police – and I had offered up a sincere prayer to God that I would be assigned to her. Once again, my prayer had been answered. As for *Ben*, although we soon bonded, he had both veterinary and emotional issues. He was, I think, heartbroken to have lost his previous handler, and I had to spend a lot of time motivating him to perform his job. Tracy's dog, *Digby*, was the complete opposite, always full of energy and keen to work.

The daily training routine started with washing down the kennels, and was followed by dog exercise. After this there were classes in grooming, dog husbandry, and the 'business' of the unit. At the end of the course, to my pleasure and relief, *Ben* and I were paired with Tracy and *Digby*. In the event, we made a very effective team.

On one particular day, the Drug Squad asked for us to be sent to Paradise Village, a small community on the south coast, set in the heart of the tourist district. Intelligence had been received that somewhere in Paradise Village there was a drug storage and distribution centre, and we were tasked with finding it. During an extensive search, we discovered a few bales of marijuana, but not the main stash, and were about to return to the station in our vans, which were parked outside an old lady's house. As I climbed into my vehicle, the old lady leaned out of a window and started ranting on at me about 'duppies' under her house every night, and demanding what I was going to do about them. I should explain that, in Bajan folklore, duppies are the spirits of the dead, and they are *very* real to the older generation. Clearly, what she needed was not a policeman but the local Obeah woman. I was about to make a polite excuse when I had an idea, which I shared with Tracy.

Moments later, with the two dogs, we were under the old lady's house, where we found a huge stash of marijuana, which turned out to be worth around 4 million US Dollars. At the time, it was the largest haul ever made on the island. Back at the station, with our uniforms filthy from crawling around under the house and reeking of marijuana, we were congratulated for a job well done. Shortly after that, on the annual Commissioner's Parade, we were commended for 'going above and beyond the call of duty'. This was not my only success.

Some weeks later, *Ben* and I were at the airport, engaged in patrolling the lines of departing and arriving passengers, looking for a 'passive find' – in other words, searching for drugs about which we had not already been alerted. *Ben* was on good form that day and identified an American passenger, who had just arrived from Montego Bay in Jamaica and was waiting to clear customs. I asked her if she was carrying any illegal drugs, and without hesitating, she reached into a pocket and handed over a small packet of weed. I arrested her on the spot, and she was later charged and convicted of being in possession of, and importing, illegal drugs. Had the packet been larger, she would probably have been charged with dealing. It was my first and only passive find and I was given a big round of applause when I got back to the station. With these successes, and the fact that I got to spend a lot of time at the airport, I was in heaven and couldn't have been happier. But I wasn't content. What was I to do?

CHAPTER 3

The Beat of a Distant Drum

OVER THE COMING DAYS, I talked matters over with Marketha and Terry, and we came to the conclusion that there was more to life than being a policeman in Barbados. Both Terry and I decided that we needed to look for an opportunity to grow. So having got ourselves to a peak of fitness, but without telling my dad or any of our colleagues at work, we applied for the Royal Marines selection course in England. In 2004, we used our four weeks' annual leave to undergo this challenge.

For me, this started with a pre-selection fitness test in Derby (where I was staying with my Uncle Fitz), which I passed easily. I then went to the Commando Training Centre Royal Marines at Lympstone in Devon, where I was subjected to three days of psychological and physical tests, ending with a mile-and-a-half run, during which the PT instructors 'beasted' us rotten. And the end result? I was accepted for training with the Royal Marines. Then something happened.

Back in Derby, I had a vivid dream one night in which I saw my dad sitting in the front house at home; next to him was a dark figure, who then got up and left. For some reason, I knew that my dad was dying and that the figure next to him was Death. Then I heard a voice telling me that if I joined the military, I too would die. Shortly after this, my leave was up and I flew back to Barbados. On that flight, I decided to put the Royal Marines on the back burner. With my dad ill and probably dying, my priorities were to support my mum and not upset him. This meant forgetting (for the time being) the idea of joining the British Armed Forces, and fully re-engaging with my police job. Before I left for England, there had been talk of *Ben* being retired and me being given a new dog. That at least was something to look forward to.

When I got home, it was clear that my father was fading. In the month that I had been away, he had become increasingly frail and his memory was deteriorating. This had put a great strain on my mum, but at least we were on hand to support her. Although Marketha and I had started our married life in a rented house, when it seemed likely that I would be away in England for an extended period, we had moved back to my parents' house with our daughter Erin.

So we were all under the same roof when one night, a couple of months after I had returned from Derby, my dad collapsed in the bathroom. I jumped out of bed and found Sissy and my mum with him. We picked him up and managed to get him back to his bed, and then mum called an ambulance. He was struggling to speak, and I reckoned that he had probably suffered a massive stroke. As we waited for help to arrive, mum rubbed his chest with alcohol and he seemed to revive a bit. At last, the ambulance pulled up outside the house, dad was loaded into it, and mum and Sissy went with him to the Queen Elizabeth Hospital, while the rest of us went back to bed.

The following day, mum called and asked me to bring some of dad's clothes to the hospital. She also said that he seemed a bit better, and had asked to see me and Jackie. When I got to the A&E ward, I was astonished at his condition: he seemed to be years younger, his face had filled out, and he looked really good. As I stood to one side, he told Jackie that he loved her, was proud of her, and not to let anyone get between her and Alvin. Then he called me to him. Having told me that he loved me, he said he knew that he had been hard on me in the past, but that it had been done with love and because he wanted only the best for me. We then hugged each other. It was a very strange moment, but it was only afterwards that I realised he was saying goodbye. Fully expecting to see him the next day, I left the hospital and went straight into work.

Later that night, the hospital called and asked mum to get there as quickly as she could. Although I was very tired, I drove her into Bridgetown. The mood in the car was subdued, made more so by the fact that there seemed to be nothing but sad music on the radio. Mum didn't say much, and I don't think she was surprised when we arrived at the hospital to find that dad had died. He was lying in a bed in a regular ward and looked really peaceful. Mum stroked his face and said quietly: 'Mappie, go with God – we will be alright here.' I said nothing, for I was completely numb.

I got home early in the morning, crawled into bed with Marketha and Erin, and cried for about five minutes; but that was the full extent of my visible emotions. It wasn't that I didn't care, I did. However, I also realised that my dad's death was both a tragedy and a blessing for my mum. Having cared for him for such a long time, at the expense of her own life, she could now get on with living. I also knew that he was at peace, and having said what he needed to before the end, had died a happy man. Later that morning, the family came together at my mum's house and someone called my dad's brother Burkley in the UK to give him the sad news. Marketha, despite being pregnant with our second child, was an absolute tower of strength, particularly with my family who are not always easy.

A few days later, dad was buried in Saint John's Parish Churchyard next to his relations in a ceremony that was every bit as 'cool' as he was. It was a very sad event, shared by family, friends, and my former colleagues in the RRU; even Sergeant McGeary and Tracy Bridgeman were there. But I showed no outward grief, for all my grieving had been internalised. I was also grappling with a problem. Although Terry and I had told no one at work of our plans, news had leaked out. It quickly became clear to me from remarks around the office and elsewhere that my bid to join the Royal Marines was causing me real problems.

The first that I knew of this formally was when I turned up at the station for an 11 a.m. to 7 p.m. shift shortly after my dad had died. 'Leave your dog in the kennels and go to the office,' the duty sergeant told me, when I reported to the desk. In the Canine Unit office, I found Sergeant McGeary and Tracy waiting for me, and looking grim. 'We understand,' he said, 'that you are not committed to the unit for the long-term, so your services are no longer required in Canine and you will be transferred back to the SSU.' That was it: no discussion and no appeal. I felt both hurt and betrayed by Tracy, who should at the very least have discussed it with me or given me a warning of what was headed my way.

On the shift that followed, I was on an operation with the Drug Squad. When we returned to the station, I was chatting to some of their guys when the subject of my transfer out of Canine came up. It quickly emerged that they were really angry I was being posted back to the SSU. That made at least two of us. Beside the fact that no one had bothered to consult me about my intentions, and if they had I would have told them that I was once again fully committed to the police. It was damned unfair. I worked as hard, if not harder, than anyone else in the unit; and I had received two commendations for jobs well done. Now, without any discussion, I was being sent to the SSU, a unit about which I already had severe reservations, which had led me to transfer to Canine in the first place. The year 2004 was turning out to be awful, but worse was yet to come.

Given that my dad had died and I was being thrown out of the Canine Unit, my idea of joining the Royal Marines once again re-surfaced. I made contact with the Training Centre at Lympstone, only to be told that my application had gone time-expired. If I wanted to join, I would have to go through the pre-selection and selection process all over again. That was not an option I was willing to consider. However, despite this setback, I did not completely dismiss the idea of joining the British Armed Forces. I had never forgotten watching the Foot Guards at Buckingham Palace. Was that a possibility, I wondered? To try and get an answer to that question, I contacted the British High Commission in Bridgetown and asked to speak to someone about joining the British Army.

I was called in for a meeting with the Military Attaché, who happened to be an officer in the Household Cavalry. I told him what had occurred with the Royal Marines, and of my childhood dream of becoming a Foot

Guard. He said that at twenty-four I was a bit old to be joining the infantry, '... but the Household Cavalry would probably take you,' he added. 'What do they do?' I asked. In answer, he showed me a short video of armoured cars charging across the Canadian prairie – and I was hooked.

However, before I could do anything about it, in early September Hurricane Ivan devastated Grenada, where a member of my family was living. I immediately put my own problems to one side, and headed off there to help with the recovery. While in Grenada, I thought more about the meeting at the High Commission, and I came to the conclusion – despite my gut telling me otherwise – that I owed it to myself and to the police to try and make a go of the SSU, before seeing if the Household Cavalry would have me.

Although I had some good friends in the SSU, over the next few weeks, it became clear that the unit itself didn't really want me. Was this because they knew that I had applied to join the Royal Marines? Was it because of my ejection from the Canine Unit? Or did they simply have a problem with me? I honestly didn't and still don't know the answer. What I do know is that I was sent on no courses, as I might reasonably have expected, and I heard mutterings about my bravery. That said, Station Sergeant Walker, and my three shift sergeants – Alvin Chandler, Fred Clarke and Sergeant Spooner – were all good blokes and gave me lots of support. My problems, it would emerge, lay with other SSU officers and one in particular.

My time in the SSU was not, however, without its bizarre moments of black humour. On Exercise TRADE WINDS, a training day which was designed to test our skills in a range of civil emergencies, I was part of a riot control unit that included policemen armed variously with shields, CS gas, baton rounds, and M-16 rifles. I was in the CS-gas Section, standing next to PC Gladstone Worrell, a big, burly guy, and PC Kevin Green (a good friend who, not much later, was killed during a shoreline drugs operation). The exercise situation was a simulated riot and the SSU's job was to disperse it. At one moment, the CS-gas Section was ordered forward, beyond the line of shield-carrying constables, to 'fire' tear gas and so disperse the crowd.

This was an *exercise*, but it was being conducted in a crowded suburb of Bridgetown, outside a supermarket and near to a main road. When Station Sergeant Walker ordered us to 'fire' we did so, using live CS rounds. The chaos that followed was immense. 'What the hell do you think you're doing?' Station Sergeant Walker yelled at Kevin. He replied: 'You told us to fire, so we fired'. At this Walker went ballistic and the inspector in overall charge took off like Concorde. The improper use of CS gas aside, 2005 started on a high note for me with the birth of our second daughter Jodie on 26th January. It wasn't until 29th March that my world changed forever.

The SSU is an armed unit, and like all such units its members are required to undergo frequent weapons training and achieve annual firearms-handling certification. On this particular occasion, the shoot was being run by the SSU officer with whom I'd disagreed over the cock-fighting operation back in 2003. He accused me of behaving dangerously, pulled me off the ranges, told me that I had failed my certification, and ordered me to surrender my weapons.

The following day, my shift was deployed to patrol the Oistins Fish Festival, an annual cultural event at which the local fishermen showed off their catches and their skills, and there is a lot of partying. In Barbados, partying can lead to trouble, and so our patrol was armed as usual. Despite having lost my sidearms, I was issued with a pistol, albeit it without a holster or a lanyard, which meant that I had to keep a firm hold on it for the whole of our patrol. Although there was no real trouble, I did not have an easy time of it, given that I was in constant danger of having my weapon snatched from me.

The next morning, the officer who had stripped me of my right to carry firearms told me that I would have to go on patrols unarmed, until I had retrained and been re-certified. In the UK that may not be an issue, but in Barbados it is. 'But I carried a pistol yesterday,' I protested, 'without it I have no way of protecting myself.' In reply, he said that if I was so worried about my personal safety then I could drive for Sergeant Spooner. It was meant as an insult, and I took it as one. 'Don't worry, Mappie,' Spooner said to me, when I joined him at his vehicle, 'you'll be OK.' With that we got into his Land Rover and started our patrol in Bridgetown, which passed off without incident.

As we were returning to the SSU base at District A Station, we saw a large column of smoke rising from Glendairy Prison, which was located almost opposite our base. No sooner had we seen it than the radio crackled into life: 'Mike-Two-Four,' that was our vehicle, 'return to Sierra-Sierra-Uniform immediately.' On our arrival back at Station Hill, we were told that we would form the first response to what was an all-out prison riot, and were ordered to get into whatever riot gear we could lay our hands on. Quickly pulling on shin pads and helmets, five of us were then driven over to the prison gates, where we were let in by the prison guards.

Inside, the prison was a scene of pure chaos. There were 997 prisoners on the loose, stabbing and slashing with knives at anyone (fellow inmates included) who crossed their paths, and the entire prison building was going up in flames. Outside the heat was thirty-five degrees, inside it was considerably hotter and very dangerous. I was paired with my friend Gladstone Worrell; but we both knew that our powers of independent action terminated as we crossed into the prison courtyard. Once inside, we could only act at the request or order of a prison guard.

Almost immediately Gladstone was confronted by a huge Rastafarian, who pushed him in the chest. But as we had no orders, there was nothing that he could do about it and even if I had wanted to intervene, I was completely unarmed. Thank God, it wasn't too long before we were withdrawn back to the station, where we were given the time to get into full riot gear, including gas masks. I was not, however, issued with a weapon. When I protested, the officer who had stripped me of my side arms and certification handed me a wooden truncheon, which was about as much use as an ice lolly in Hell.

Back once again in the prison, one of the main reasons that I survived the next few minutes was because SSU Constable Gregory Cadogan, knowing that I was unarmed and at considerable personal risk, deliberately put himself between me and the rioters. His bravery was not, however, the end of my troubles. I can't be sure, but I think that around this time CS gas was fired to gain control of the riot. There was certainly gas in the air; but when I pulled on my gas mask, I quickly found that it was defective and for some reason I couldn't breathe. Standing next to me was Commander Aquinas Clarke, who could see that I was having difficulties. 'Mappie, are you OK?' he asked. 'No,' I replied, 'I can't breathe in this mask.' 'Give it to me,' he ordered. He held it to his face, looked up at the Station Sergeant, who was acting as a sniper on a tower, and then chucked it to the ground. 'Go back to the station and get yourself sorted out.'

By the time I got there, my face was on fire from a toxic mixture of sweat and CS gas, and my clothes were soaked through with perspiration. I staggered up to the first-floor balcony overlooking the station's courtyard, where Constable Kay Read saw me and promptly poured a jug of cold water over my head. At that moment, the officer who had earlier given me the truncheon came into the yard and looked up, to see Kay rubbing my shoulders. 'If you can't handle the work, Mapp – fucking leave!' There and then I decided to take him at his word.

The next morning, I was assigned to desk duties, where I used the time to write my letter of resignation. I then told the Station Sergeant that I wanted to go to Central and collect a flexibility allowance that was due to me. 'Sure, Mappie, no problem. Take one of the cars from the pool, and could you drop off this correspondence for me while you are there,' he added, handing me some envelopes. Half-an-hour later at Central, I sought out the inspector in charge of Human Resources. Fortunately, I knew him well, as he had been one of my first sergeants. 'Can I see you for a moment, sir?' I asked. 'Sure, Mappie, come in and sit down. What's on your mind?' 'This is my resignation, sir,' I said, handing him my letter, 'but I would prefer that it stayed between you and me for as long as possible.' 'So, SSU don't know about this?' 'No, sir.' 'Alright. Level with me – what's the problem?' 'I really don't want to talk about it, sir. All you need to know is that I've had my fill and it's time to move on.'

'I see . . . ' he said, 'but if you have a *real* grievance, I need to know about it, as it may affect others.' 'I'm sorry, sir, but I really don't want to talk about it.' 'OK. But people are going to ask why.' He paused. 'Instead of resigning, stay on for the few months left to complete your five-year engagement, then retire and collect your pension.' 'I can't do that, sir.' 'It's that bad?' 'Yes, I'm afraid it is. I want to leave as soon as I can.' 'You know that if you change your mind, you can re-join within the year?' 'I won't be coming back, sir.' 'Very well. I can't say that I'm happy about this – and you'll have to serve out your three months' notice. In the meantime, keep your head down.' 'I will, sir. Can you keep this quiet?' He said nothing to this, but the SSU only found out a week before I was due to leave.

No sooner had I handed in my resignation than two things happened: I felt as if a huge weight had been lifted from my shoulders, and I immediately started the long process of applying to join the British Army, which took most of the three months that I had left to serve in the Royal Barbados Police Force.

When the news broke that I was leaving, there was a mixture of good and bad reactions. A sergeant who didn't like me asked why I had been so secretive, but Sergeant Fred Clarke said: 'I know you've had a rough time, but I hope I wasn't a contributor.' 'No,' I said, 'you are one of the good guys.' 'Well, I'm sad you couldn't discuss it with me – and I'm sad you are leaving.' 'Thank you,' I replied, 'but I think it's the best for everyone.' It wasn't long before Tracy heard the news and came to talk to me about it, but I wouldn't engage with her.

On my last day, the Station Sergeant took me to one side and started off by saying that it was a pity I hadn't discussed it with him. 'For a young man like you to take such a decision, something must be wrong. I couldn't be sorrier that this happened here and under these conditions. Well, I wish you all the best and I hope that you stay in touch.' 'That won't be easy. I'm leaving the country tomorrow.' And that is exactly what I did.

Sissy flew to England with me. After landing at Gatwick, we made our way to Uncle Fitz's house in Derby. I had very little money, and I won't pretend that the months that followed were easy. They weren't, and they were made even harder by my uncle. It was, therefore, with some relief that in mid-October I finally cleared the last hurdle in my journey to becoming a British soldier and received my joining instructions. I was told to report to the Army Training Centre at Pirbright to start fourteen weeks of recruit training. The next phase of my life was about to start.

CHAPTER 4

A Donkey-Walloper in Khaki

AT 6 A.M. ON THURSDAY 17th November 2005, my Uncle Fitz took me to Derby station and saw me onto the train for London. I carried with me everything that I possessed; I was leaving Derby with no regrets, and as I wasn't about to look back, I don't know if he waited to wave me off. As I settled into my seat, I felt both liberated from what I had left behind, but also apprehensive as to what was to come.

I knew that aged twenty-four, I was at the upper-age limit of Army recruiting and the intense cold of that November day did not help matters; particularly as I also knew that it would only get colder during basic training. 'Only God knows how I'm going to get through this,' I thought. Anyway, I took a few deep breaths, put my worries to the back of my mind, and tried to enjoy the journey to St Pancras. From there I took a tube to Waterloo, where I boarded a train for Brookwood in Surrey.

It was only when I got onto the platform at my destination, I realised that there was a carriageful of other lads also headed for the Army Training Centre (ATC), Pirbright. This was no longer the famous Guards Depot, but one of the Army's centres for what is currently called the Common Military Syllabus, a fourteen-week course in basic military skills under-taken by all Army recruits.

As I looked around at the other lads, I couldn't help noticing that most of them were much younger than me, and that almost all of them were white. But it was clear that we were all in the same boat, which broke down some of the barriers. As we were shown onto a bus outside by the waiting Non-Commissioned Officers (NCOs), the usual British reserve in the presence of strangers fell away, and the chat amongst us became fairly general. I had expected lots of barked orders, but although they were strict, there was no yelling by the ATC's NCOs on the platform and in fact we were all made to feel very welcome during the short drive to the camp. As the bus drove through the main gates, I couldn't help thinking that I was passing the point of no return. 'This is going to be OK,' I reassured myself, not for the first or last time.

The discipline that I had been expecting didn't remain hidden for very long. No sooner had we got off the bus than we were lined up, our names were taken, and we were assigned to training Troops. I was put in one of four Sections of Sphynx Troop of 59 (Asten) Battery, part of 1 Army Training Regiment (1ATR) in which were recruits for the Royal Artillery (RA), the Royal Logistic Corps (RLC) and the Household Cavalry. The Battery Commander was Captain Les Kibble of The Blues and Royals, a former regimental Quartermaster and an instructor at the Royal Military Academy Sandhurst; our Troop Leader was Captain Nana Twumasi-Ankrah, also a Blue and Royal, who was known to everyone as 'Captain TA'. He is now a lieutenant colonel and, until recently, was The Queen's Equerry). The Troop Sergeant was Sergeant Norris and our Section Commander was Bombardier Robby Reynolds, both of the RA. Two of the other Section Commanders were Lance Corporal of Horse (LCoH) Donovan Mowatt of The Life Guards and Bombardier Fayanne Julian, another member of the RA.

Having been assigned to a Troop, in which I was the only black recruit (although Captain TA was a Ghanaian and LCoH Mowatt was of mixed-race), we were then shown to a two-story barrack block, where our Section was assigned a barrack room on the first floor, in which we were invited to choose a bed. I took one between Nigel Hawkins, destined like me for the Household Cavalry, and Gareth Igo, who was joining the Royal Logistic Corps; he was very young and scared of his own shadow. We bonded quickly and for the whole course we had each other's back.

Having dumped our civvy stuff, we were then herded off to the Quarter-master's (QM) stores to draw our military kit. Shortly after this, all the lads destined for the Household Cavalry were lined up. Captain Kibble, who it was immediately clear – as an ex-Warrant Officer – was not a man to be messed with, asked us if we had a regimental preference. I should explain at this point that the Household Cavalry, known to the rest of the Army as 'the Donkey Wallopers', is formed of the two most senior Regiments in the British Army: The Life Guards (who in Full Dress wear red tunics and white helmet plumes); and The Blues and Royals (who wear blue tunics and red helmet plumes). Until 1991, these two Regiments operated autono-mously within the Household Cavalry as operational armoured units, and each contributed a horsed/ceremonial Squadron to the Household Cavalry Mounted Regiment (HCMR) at Hyde Park Barracks in London. In 1991, the independent armoured units were merged (actually, it was called a 'union') to form the Household Cavalry Regiment (HCR). So from that date on, although officers and men are *members* of either The Life Guards or The Blues and Royals, and wear distinctively different uniforms and cap badges, they *serve* in HCR and HCMR. This is a source of endless confusion to everyone outside the Household Cavalry.

As Captain Kibble stood in front of us, he asked if anyone had a prefer-ence as to Regiment. One lad, called Duggan, said that he wanted to be a Blue and Royal, and the rest of us just looked blank; all I knew was that I wanted to drive a Household Cavalry light tank across the Canadian prairie. So, Captain Kibble walked along the rank and assigned us alternately to each Regiment. As he passed me, he said 'red', which meant that I was now a Life Guard, the first Barbadian member of the Regiment formed by King Charles II while in exile in the 1650s, and known as 'The Tins' because of the cuirasses (steel breast and back plates) worn in Full Dress.

Back in the barrack room, Captain TA arrived and introduced himself. He made it very clear from the outset that he wanted teamwork. In particular, he expected us to look out for and help each other. It was immediately clear to me that Captain TA was a born leader, and he quickly became my role model. From the outset, he was not only inspirational, but he also got us to bond as a unit. One of his techniques was drawn from the movie *Gladiator*, starring Russell Crowe. Captain TA would come into a room and shout, 'Gladiator', to which every member of his Troop would reply in unison, 'On my signal, unleash hell!' Set down in black and white here, it sounds a bit childish, but at the time it really worked as a way of uniting us into a single entity. It also set us apart from the rest of the recruit troops. It wasn't long before none of us, and particularly me, wanted to be the one to let him down. Our Section Commander, Bombardier Reynolds, also made an immediate impression on us, and gave me the confidence to tell him of my old groin injury and my worry that I wouldn't be able to keep up. 'Don't worry, Corie,' he said, 'I won't let you fall behind.'

In some respects, I was well ahead of the other recruits, thanks to my time in the Cadets, the Royal Barbados Police Force and the Barbados Defence Force Reserves. I knew how to polish boots and press uniforms; I knew about barrack room tidiness and I knew the basics of drill, map reading, and weapon handling. The first of these advantages led to me stocking up with Mr Sheen polish, spray starch – and pressing thirty-two pairs of trousers on that first and very long night! I also had no trouble with locker layouts and bed-making, both of which are important features of recruit training.

In addition to these personal chores, we had to keep our barrack room, the corridor on the first floor, and the washroom we used in a constantly gleaming state. To achieve this, and to ensure that the daily inspections of our kit, lockers, beds and accommodation did not turn into moments of high anxiety, we quickly worked out a routine and then implemented it as a team from the get-go (start). Inevitably, there was one idiot who refused to muck-in and I had to have words with him; not surprisingly, he did not complete the course. Meanwhile, the Section housed on the ground floor below us did not follow our lead, as a result of which things there ran less smoothly.

Before turning in that night, I called home and reassured Marketha that all was well. The next morning, training started in earnest. On parade at 5 a.m. we were inspected, given white fabric slides (denoting a trainee) to put on the front of our combat kit, and then marched to breakfast. After that there was a series of lectures, starting with one on equality and diversity, which made clear they were important features of the British Army in the twenty-first century. When I arrived at Pirbright I was the only recruit with a moustache, but no one told me to shave it off. A couple of days later, it emerged in conversation that this was because my instructors had assumed that it had some sort of religious significance to me. When I said that wasn't the case, I was told in no uncertain terms to get rid of it. If I remember rightly, the actual words used were: 'In that case, Mapp, tomorrow you won't have that piece of shit on your mush.' Clearly, a purely decorative piece of face furniture was not covered by 'equality and diversity'.

After the introductory talks, we had to undergo a fitness test, which began with a run. I was anxious about this, but Bombardier Reynolds ran with me and I had no problems. However, he could not help me with the next part of the test, which involved carrying jerry cans filled with sand. For this, we were under the command of a PTI (Physical Training Instructor) from the Royal Regiment of Scotland. Unfortunately, I was the first to take on the task and I couldn't understand a single word he was saying, so thick was his accent. He was the first Scotsman I had ever met. Needless to say, he started yelling at me. Keeping my cool, I replied, as politely and respectfully as I could: 'I'm really, really sorry, but I don't understand a word that you are saying.' At that, everyone fell about laughing, including the PTI. Then, as if talking to a baby, he very slowly explained what he wanted me to do. 'Do you understand now, laddie?' I said that I did, and then got on with the task. While on the subject of accents, Bombardier Reynolds had a trick of asking each of us to remember a fact. Mine was the name of a town in Newfoundland, Canada. For some reason, he found that the way I pronounced it was hilarious and he would ask the question whenever he wanted to generate a laugh. 'What's your important fact, Corie?' he would demand. 'There is a town in Newfoundland, Canada, called Dildo, Bombardier,' I would shout back, as everyone around me collapsed.

47

Next on the programme was drill. While I had been happy to demon-strate and share my experience of kit cleaning and barrack room house-keeping with the other lads, I decided that it would bring me no credit to let on that I was reasonably experienced at basic drill. Looking back, I may have fooled my fellow trainees, but I don't think that I fooled the drill instructors.

On the second night we had Exercise ICEBREAKER. This was organised by Troop, and involved all the trainees and our instructors spending the night in the field. As the name implied, the purpose of this exercise was to break the ice between trainers and trainees, and to help bonding within the Troop. We were shown how to pack a Bergen rucksack with the kit we would need, and then marched off to an open space within the camp's perimeter, where we pitched some tents. On that November night it was minus-nine degrees; it was also my first experience of freezing weather in the open. Despite the fact that I had taken the precaution of putting on every bit of clothing I possessed – a fact which caused much good-natured ribbing – and we had lit a fire outside our tent, around which we all huddled, I was frozen to the core. 'Guys,' I said through numb lips, 'I'm really suffering. I joined the Army to drive tanks, not to be deep-frozen.' 'But it's *only* minus-nine,' one of them joked. 'That's OK for you,' I said, 'but I've just come from where it's always thirty-one degrees plus.' Although I was colder than I'd ever been before, I remember that as a really great night and a brilliant start to the course. We all got to know each other by exchanging personal information, and bonded through the shared discomfort.

I'm not going to record here a blow-by-blow account of my time at Pirbright, during which we were occupied from First Parade to Lights Out with drill, weapon training, PT, swimming (I was still not much good in the water), map reading, field craft and Section-level infantry tactics in the field (which I really enjoyed) interspersed with instructional talks and overnight exercises. However, I will say that it got progressively more challenging physically, as the strain on my old groin injury increased and the cold got to me. Sometimes, my left leg would go completely dead on runs, and on a couple of occasions, I either couldn't complete a run or was excused a duty because I was in the medical centre. I hated letting down my mates, and more particularly, disappointing Bombardier Reynolds. During my time at Pirbright, I made some really good friends, including Reece Foran, another Life Guard, who told me early on that whatever the Army's directives on equality and diversity, he didn't think much of black people. By the time we got to Christmas leave, he readily admitted that he had changed his mind.

At last, Christmas arrived and I headed home for the holiday, with my Bergen slung over my shoulder and accompanied by Corporal Mike Leacock of 16 Air Assault Brigade at Colchester; he was a Bajan I had met through a mutual friend in the Barbados Defence Force. I planned to keep up my fitness by yomping up and down Farley Hill, a prominent feature on the island. When I arrived, the family was really pleased to see me, and definitely proud of what I was achieving. However, my daughter Jodie didn't know who I was, as I had left home when she was only a few months old. Sissy and Jackie told me not to worry, but of course this bothered me.

Before I left Barbados to join the British Army, some in the Police said that I was jumping into the deep end of a pool without a life jacket. This analogy was appropriate, as I only passed my military swimming test at Pirbright by bouncing off the bottom of the pool, a fact which didn't fool the instructors, who thought it was funny and passed me anyway. Given these warnings, I made a point of visiting the Police, and old friends in the Reserves, to show everyone that I was surviving the training. All too soon, however, it was time to kiss the girls, Marketha, and the rest of the family goodbye, and return to the UK for the second half of the course.

The weeks after that Christmas leave seemed to pass very quickly, and included a visit to a Commonwealth War Graves site at Ypres in Belgium. After we had toured the huge cemetery, we took part in a parade at the Menin Gate, during which – thanks to my drill skills – I laid a wreath on behalf of 1ATR. Then, almost before I knew it, we were on the final exercise of our training, which took place over three days in torrential rain on Pirbright Common. I had been appointed a mini-Section commander, to test my leadership skills. Captain TA kept up our morale in his own special

49

ways, which included playing *Time Goes by So Slowly* by Madonna on his mobile phone, as we stood in waterlogged slit trenches.

But I was having problems. One of my tasks on the exercise was to set up an ambush. Although it was successful, my weapon jammed a few times, which did not look good. Then, on the day before the end of the exercise, I fainted on a March & Shoot. It was my own fault; I hadn't eaten properly earlier, and then decided not to carry water with me, to lighten my pack and so take pressure off my old injury. My collapse led to my first serious bollocking from Bombardier Reynolds, who said that if I didn't perform well on the competition run the following day, I would be 'back trooped'. It was a hard lesson that I never forgot.

Thank God, I did better than expected on the competition run and Captain Kibble acknowledged this when he told me: 'Coming back from that was a good thing'. That was praise indeed. I then heard that I had been awarded the prize for best drill to be presented at the Passing Out Parade on 17th February 2006. 'I think that you drill better than me,' the battery sergeant major told me with a laugh when I next saw him. In fact, lads from the Household Cavalry had swept the board when it came to prizes; Duggan got the one for most improved recruit, and Aiden MacCauliffe, a Life Guard like me, won best recruit and best fitness.

On the day itself, and for reasons that I quite understood, none of my family were there to watch me. However, Terry Thompson, my old friend from the Royal Barbados Police Force, happened to be in the UK and accepted my invitation to attend. He had encouraged me throughout my time at Pirbright, and his presence was most appropriate as he had won the prize for best drill when we had been in police training together back home. His being there also reminded me that the sergeant who used to drill us in Bridgetown was forever talking about how the Guards had perfected drill at Pirbright.

And so, my time at the ATC came to an end, but not before I had a nasty shock, about which more in a moment. It had been tough, but it was also a very fair regime and integrity had been a key part of it all. As well as shouting 'Gladiator' to get our response, Captain TA used to shout 'C Drills', to which our response was to chant: 'Courage, Discipline, Respect, Integrity, Loyalty, Selfless Commitment.' As principles of behaviour go, they are as good as any that I know.

Which brings me to the nasty shock. Before we went on leave, Captain Kibble once again lined up the Household Cavalrymen and told us that he was proud of us. He then said that we should look forward to our next period of training, which would be with Household Cavalry Mounted Regiment (HCMR) at Hyde Park Barracks in London. At first, I thought that I had misheard him. I had joined the Household Cavalry to drive armoured vehicles, not to ride horses, and I queried the posting. 'Every soldier in the Household Cavalry starts on horses, Mapp,' he replied. And that was it.

. . .

Early one morning two weeks later, straight off a flight from Barbados, I arrived at the gate on the Knightsbridge side of HCMR's barracks and rang the bell. At first nothing happened, then a Lance Corporal, who introduced himself as Tariq Baskh, appeared at the gate and asked me what I wanted. 'I'm here for mounted training,' I replied. 'Then you'd better come in,' he said, with a really friendly smile.

As I'd come straight from Gatwick, I was very early and well ahead of the other recruits. So, while I waited in the Guard Room, I reflected on the fact that, having completed basic training, I couldn't be sent back. However, the challenges that lay ahead of me were awesome, particularly as I had never before done more than pat a horse's nose. At last, the other recruits arrived, including Reece Foran, and we were soon joined by the Ride NCO, who had driven up from Combermere Barracks in Windsor, in a minibus that was to take us there.

Our mounted training was divided into two phases. The first was the Khaki Ride, so called because we would wear our khaki No 2 Dress, rather than Blues or Full Dress. This took place at Windsor, lasted for six weeks, and involved teaching us how to ride, as well as stable management, grooming, tack cleaning, and cavalry drill – both mounted and dismounted. Because we were starting in the spring, our Khaki Ride would end at HCMR's Summer Camp at Bodney in Norfolk. After some leave, we would then undergo the two-week Kit Ride at Hyde Park Barracks, which would teach us all the additional skills we needed to take part in Public Duties and State Ceremonial. This included not only the challenge of wearing Full Dress, but also all the skills and techniques to clean both our own uniforms and the equipment for our horses. At the end of the Kit Ride, there was a Pass Off Parade.

On that first day, before we left Hyde Park Barracks, we had to draw the kit we would need for the Khaki Ride. This involved going down into the bowels of the barracks where the Full Dress and Quartermaster's stores were located. An hour or so later, I emerged back into the light, staggering under the weight of a ceremonial steel helmet, a sword, and loads of other riding kit and accoutrements. Before we piled onto the minibus, we were told that during our mounted training, we would be known as Egypt Ride. I later found out that this commemorated the Household Cavalry's famous moonlight charge at Kassassin in Egypt on 28th August 1882. Its proud, and sometimes unusual, history is important to the Household Cavalry.

Within the hour we were at Combermere Barracks, where we were shown into a twelve-man barrack room and then given details of the training programme. This was to start every morning at 6 a.m. with mucking out the stables, followed by breakfast, a change into riding kit, First Parade with our horses and then into the Riding School. After lunch there was more training, including kit cleaning, and some sport.

After the initial briefing, we were shown around the camp, followed by an introduction to the skills that we would need: mucking out, tack cleaning, tacking up a horse, and so on. On that first day we were not introduced to our horses (known in the Household Cavalry as 'blacks', on account of their colour); that happened on the second morning. My horse was called *Drummond*. I soon found out that he was a reasonably easy ride at walk, trot and canter, but he was a very jerky jumper and known to be 'five-footed'. He also hated State kit, but that lay in the future.

The Household Cavalry's Riding Staff were led by the Riding Master, Captain (later Major) Dicky Waygood. We didn't see much of him on the Khaki Ride, but heard that he was incredibly fierce, although very fair, and had a wonderful way with horses. He is now the Performance Director of Britain's Olympic Eventing team, having served as Chef d'Equipe of the British Dressage team that won gold medals at the 2012 and 2016 Olympic Games. Our more immediate bosses were the Training Officer, Captain Rob Gibbs, and Squadron Corporal Major (SCM) Gardner; the riding instructor for the Khaki Ride, Lance Corporal of Horse (LCoH) Jamie Broom; the Egypt Ride Corporal of Horse (CoH) Toby, who was very eccentric and full of stories of his time on active service in Bosnia; and the two more junior Egypt Ride NCOs, Lance Corporals (LCpl) Elliot Cooper and Eddie Doyle.

In order for us to achieve a good deep seat on a horse, the training in the Riding School started with riding bareback; actually, we rode on a brown blanket strapped in place over the horse's back with a surcingle (strap). I wasn't scared, but I was certainly apprehensive when I first got on *Drummond*'s back. After all, it was the first time that I had ever sat on a horse, let alone a huge cavalry black, the top of whose shoulder (withers) was just above my head. However, the horses knew the drills much better than we ever would, and as they walked in single file around the school, I started to relax. By the end of the third day, I was in a lot of pain, from using muscles that I didn't know existed, but I was also really surprised at how much I liked riding.

Over the following weeks, we learned to control the horses at all their different paces and progressed from bareback to riding with saddles. We also learned the various manoeuvres in a group that comprise Mounted Drills, which enable a cavalry commander to move a body of men and horses into the various formations required for ceremonial events and on the battlefield in the past. It was like synchronised swimming on horses. On a couple of occasions, we were joined by Cornet Harry Wales (now HRH The Duke of Sussex), who was serving with HCR, but at this time I didn't get to talk to him.

We took bets on who would be the first to fall off, and I wasn't the first. However, once we started jumping, I had more than my fair share of falls, and once caught my foot in the stirrup and was dragged the length of the Riding School. *Drummond*'s so-called five legs, were a particular problem when we jumped poles with our hands on our heads, while reciting our name, rank and number. In fact, this exercise became such a problem for me that I seriously thought I might not Pass Off the Khaki Ride. I was saved from this fate by our move to Bodney Camp.

Even when picking myself up from yet another fall, I really enjoyed the Khaki Ride. I even got used to the weird experience of being the Night Stable Guard. On that duty, I was on my own in the stables with the horses, and solely responsible for them should anything go wrong, which it often did, horses being horses. Those nights on guard were alternately interesting and scary, but they also gave me lots of time to think. As I'd done during police training in Barbados, I often watched the aeroplanes flying in and out of Heathrow; the sight of the blinking lights on the wings and tails actually kept me sane during those long night hours. I'm so flying mad that I should add that when I wasn't staying the weekend with an aunt and uncle in Peckham, I would sometimes take myself off to the airport, so that I could just sit and watch the aeroplanes.

In the summer we moved to Bodney Camp in Norfolk, a former wartime RAF and USAF station with low concrete buildings and temporary stabling for the horses, into which HCMR moves every year for Summer Camp. This annual migration was both a sort of holiday for the horses and men, and an opportunity to carry out equestrian and military training that was not possible in London. In order to get there, we had to get our blacks into their travelling kit and then persuade them into the horse boxes, which was an interesting exercise in itself.

On arrival at Bodney, we settled the horses in their loose boxes, and then were briefed on the programme for Summer Camp. This included lots of cross-country jumping, long hacks in the countryside, and learning the sport of tent pegging. We also received instruction on dismounted cavalry drill (quite different to the foot drill taught at Pirbright), during which we had to master the art of not tripping over our swords, and wearing a helmet so that the plume remained around it – you have to keep your chin tucked in. Then there was a trip to the beach at Holkham with the horses, including an extended dip with them in the North Sea; a visit to RAF Lakenheath; and a conventional military exercise, for which Egypt Ride would act as the enemy.

As far as the cross-country jumping was concerned, I was still having problems with *Drummond*. I was really grateful when the Riding Master taught me to rise in the saddle during the approach to a jump, which helped a lot, although I never won the unofficial time trials being run by the officers. I loved the long, early morning country hacks, as did the horses, and it was during these that I really got to know our instructors. I even managed to master the art of tent pegging back in camp. I found dismounted cavalry drill on the small tarmac square very easy, as it involved no foot stamping. The Foot Guards think it's a really lazy drill, but they don't have to wear the Household Cavalry's State kit. Swimming the horses off the beach at Holkham was nothing less than amazing, although as a poor swimmer I had the genuine fear of being trampled into the sea bed by a cavalry black. If the North Sea was cool, in every sense of the word, then the visit to RAF Lakenheath, home of the USAF 48th Fighter Wing, where we were in sight of the latest F-15E/Strike Eagle fighters, was cooler still. And as for the conventional military exercise? Well, let's just say that we got battered – but it was great.

All too soon, it was time to leave Norfolk, but not before Egypt Ride was Passed Off. That was both a relief and an achievement for me. Once back at Windsor, we were given two-weeks leave, which would be followed by our move to Hyde Park Barracks for the two-week Kit Ride. As before, I took off for Barbados. This time Reece Foran and his girlfriend Chloe came with me.

In Barbados, I loved being able to show Reece and Chloe where I had been born and raised; I even took them to Farley Hill, where I trained while on leave from Pirbright. Reece in his turn loved the island. In fact, he loved the sunny climate rather too much, as I found out on the second day when Chloe took me to their hotel room, where Reece was laid out on their bed looking like a freshly cooked lobster covered in yoghurt. Fortunately, his sunburn didn't prevent him from enjoying the sights and the sea, or from telling me that he planned to propose to Chloe as soon as we had Passed Off Kit Ride.

When our leave was up, I returned to the UK with Marketha, Erin and Jodie to a semi-furnished flat in Stillington Street, Victoria. Once we were settled in, the plan was that my mother was to join us to look after the girls so that Marketha could get a job. Meanwhile, I had to say goodbye to my family in Barbados; Sissy's husband, Wayne, got very emotional and started weeping.

Our flight to Gatwick was late, which meant that I had twenty-six unanswered calls on my telephone, all from SCM Foster at Combermere, and each one progressively more abusive than the last. Putting it mildly, it seemed that my delayed return was holding up the move of Egypt Ride to London. It was not a good start, soon made worse by the bare state of our flat and the cold weather, for which Marketha and the girls were quite unprepared.

CHAPTER 5

A Tin in the Kit

HYDE PARK BARRACKS – or Knightsbridge as it is known to anyone who has served there – was my base for the next two years. Built to a design by Sir Basil Spence in the late 1960s, as a replacement for the crumbling Victorian cavalry barracks on the site, Knightsbridge is the London home of the Household Cavalry, and has been occupied by the Household Cavalry Mounted Regiment (HCMR) since 1946. Whatever the current building's design merits or otherwise, the site houses all the Household Cavalry's horses on two floors, HQ Household Division's horses, a veterinary yard, an indoor riding school, a gym, and all HCMR's administrative offices, stores, and meeting rooms. It also has single soldier accommodation, a medical centre, dining facilities, a shop, the NCOs Mess and the Officers Mess, a low-rise block of flats for the married officers and flats for most (but not all) of the married soldiers in the tower block. All of this is arranged around a large rectangular yard, where the Guards and Escorts form up before moving out through the Ceremonial Gate on the Hyde Park side of the barracks. Apparently, there hasn't been a single day since it opened when there hasn't been a building contractor's vehicle on site, so it's not quite as good at it looks. However, the 'old and bold', say that it's an improvement on the previous barracks, in which the soldiers' families lived over the stables and had to contend with running damp and armies of huge rats.

Even though I had an Army flat in Victoria, for the first two weeks at Knightsbridge I slept on site. After that, although I slept at the flat and commuted in every day on the bus, soldiers at Knightsbridge only had one thirty-six-hour leave pass every two weeks. This was partly because of the nature of the duties at HCMR and partly because, with the armoured Household Cavalry Regiment (HCR) at Windsor committed to overseas operations, HCMR had to plug the gaps in their nominal roll. Consequently, Knightsbridge was under-staffed for the whole time I was there. Nonetheless, the demands of Public Duties and State Ceremonial could make no allowances for our manpower shortage, so most of us were doing the work of two men.

Although still a part of Egypt Ride, on my arrival at Knightsbridge I was assigned to 3 Troop of The Life Guards' Mounted Squadron. The Commanding Officer at HCMR was Lieutenant Colonel Ralph Griffin; firm but fair, he went out of his way to make me feel at home, cracking jokes with me whenever we met. My Squadron Leader was Major David Brooks, my Troop Leader was Captain Mike Harley, and the two Troop Corporals of Horse were Bert Dukes and Lee Amos, both of whom were very different, a bit old school but also extremely supportive. A familiar face at HCMR was Captain TA, who had recently been appointed a Troop Leader in The Blues and Royals Squadron. He would often rock up in the stables while we were working, bearing boxes of doughnuts for us, irrespective of whether we were from the 'red' or the 'blue' corner. I quickly discovered that, although very hard work, Knightsbridge was a great place to be.

As at Combermere, I was assigned to a room, although this time it was a three-bedder. I then drew from the stores the rest of the ceremonial kit that I would need, both for myself and for my horse, including a temporary pair of cuirasses that were too large for me. Later, I was to be fitted with my own custom-made set. Up to the 1960s, Life Guards had to be at least six feet tall, so there wasn't a large stock of kit for soldiers like me, who was six inches shorter than that. Thanks to Bert Dukes, I was also issued with a pair of jack boots that had belonged to a 3 Troop guy who had recently been posted to HCR. He had won that year's Richmond Cup, the annual prize presented, usually by The Queen, at the Royal Windsor Horse Show to the best turned out Trooper in the Household Cavalry.

These jack boots were a proper pair of bobby-dazzlers, without a single crease on the uppers of the feet. I prayed that I didn't have to march in them. I should explain that it can take up to two hours to 'bob' (polish) a pair of jack boots for a pre-Queen's Life Guard inspection; the better the foundation on the boots, the easier and quicker they are to bob; but marching in them can flake off the finish on the foot and undo hours of hard work. This pair were immaculate. The kit issue was followed by the allocation of a Full Dress storage locker and the *very* strict instruction never to leave it unlocked. The kit, we were told, was both extremely expensive and eminently nick-able. Any losses would be deducted from our pay; I didn't need to be told twice.

Over the course of the next day or so, we learned how to clean all this stuff in a way that would not only make it gleam, but would earn us the coveted 'box men' duties on The Queen's Life Guard (usually referred to as 'Queen's'). The core duty for HCMR is to provide the daily Queen's Life Guard at Horse Guards on Whitehall. People ask, why at Whitehall and not at Buckingham Palace? The answer is that Horse Guards was the entrance to the Palace of Whitehall, until it burned down in 1698, after which the Court moved to St James's Palace. Instead of moving The King's Life Guard (as it then was), they simply turned the sentry boxes for the mounted guards to face the other way. Horse Guards remains to this day the official front gate to the royal palaces, which is why The Queen always passes through it on ceremonial occasions, such as the State Opening of Parliament. So much for the history.

The significance for us of the sentry boxes on Queen's, known simply as 'the boxes', was that the best turned out Dutymen (the term for Household Cavalrymen on duty) on the pre-Queen's inspection were awarded the boxes, while the rest had to provide the dismounted sentries. Sitting on a horse, facing onto Whitehall, and being photographed – and that wasn't all – by hundreds of tourists was an infinitely better duty than being on one's feet for an hour at a time in the Tilt Yard, or under the Horse Guards arch.

The Kit Ride was particularly hard for me, when (as I'd been warned) I discovered that *Drummond* had a hatred of State kit. To put it bluntly, he went from being a difficult horse at Windsor to being a raving lunatic in London. Like all horses, the cavalry blacks are intelligent and aware. My co-author tells me that in his day there was a Troop horse who loathed officers' Frock Coats, and would always try to kick the frock-coated Adjutant on the pre-Queen's inspection. Nothing else bothered him, just officers' Frock Coats. *Drummond* had a similar problem with Full Dress horse furniture, and I spent a lot of time picking myself up from the tan, either in the Riding School or out in the park.

Eventually, the Riding Staff realised that the problem was not me but *Drummond*, and he was sent back to Windsor. His replacement on the Kit Ride was a horse called *Yankee*, who was an absolute Rolls-Royce of a horse and never binned me. Sadly, I had to leave him behind when I joined 3 Troop, where my horses were *Blenheim*, another five-footer with a very uncomfortable trot; a huge black called *Albert*, named after Queen Victoria's husband; and later *Belize*, a really feisty mare, but an armchair ride, with four smart-as-paint white socks, dotted with black spots.

Meanwhile, Marketha and the girls were settling into our flat, which was gradually equipped with all that we needed, thanks to the generosity of friends and relations; my aunt in Peckham gave us a freezer and my uncle a fridge. Marketha acquired warm clothes for herself and the girls, and quickly got a good job with the government, Erin started school, and mum arrived to look after Jodie. Although I wasn't allowed to stay at the flat during the Kit Ride, which was hard, I did manage to meet up with Marketha for an hour or two on the occasional evening. Once I was able to sleep at home every night, I remember lying in our bedroom and looking out of the window at a building opposite, that was lit with blue lights. I don't know why, but I found that light very calming.

Back at Knightsbridge, I had to memorise the mounted drills, including the trumpet calls and the officers' sword movements (known as cutting) that signalled a change of pace or direction. I also had to master the art of riding in jack boots, which were so thick I could hardly feel the side of the horse with my leg. I also had to cope with the bulky cuirasses (in my case, still too big); and learn how to keep my helmet on at the sitting trot or the canter. For Life Guards this is not easy, as we wear the helmet's chinstrap under the lip. Blues and Royals are more fortunate, as they wear it under the chin. Why? I have no idea.

I also had to get through two major inspections before the Ride Pass Off. Preparing for these inspections was quite literally an all-night job. But we all mucked in together and made a bit of a party of it, ordering in pizzas to eat while we cleaned helmets, cuirasses, spurs, swords, and the horses' bright chains; then we bobbed all the black leather, and white-sapped the buff belts, gauntlets, sword slings, buckskin britches, and the horses' surcingles. And all of that had to be done before we started grooming the horses to make their coats and hooves shine.

Eventually, the big day dawned. Marketha, my mum and the girls were all there to watch me Pass Off. I'd come first in the Adjutant Inspection and done well in the Riding Master's Inspection, but Reece was awarded the prize for 'cleanest man'. Before we took the horses back to the stables after Pass Off, he proposed to Chloe from the saddle – and she accepted. The next day I started full time with 3 Troop. Later that week I was preparing for my first Queen's Life Guard when disaster struck during a sports evening in the gym. We were playing football, I went to tackle another Trooper, we collided and I broke my foot.

One benefit of this accident was that I got to spend more time with the family, and most days I took Erin to and from school. At work, I spent the next two weeks limping around the stables and acting as stableman to Bert Dukes. One of my duties was to tack up his horse. The first time I did this, with the whole Regiment formed up in the yard for an Escort, I failed to tighten the girth sufficiently. Bert clambered up the mounting block in Full Dress, took the reins, put his left foot in the stirrup, and swung his right leg over the saddle. The moment the left stirrup started to take his weight, the saddle began to rotate towards the underside of his horse. He could have ended up in a heap on the tarmac or worse. Needless to say, he was livid, and I felt a complete fool.

After that, things could only get better which they did. My first Queen's following the footballing accident was in October, by which time we were in what is called Cloak Order. This had the great advantage, particularly for me, that I didn't have to wear my overly-large cuirasses, as the huge cloaks – actually very full-skirted coats – covered us from chin to ankle, and so the burden of kit cleaning was somewhat reduced.

The day started at 6.30 a.m. with GuardEx, when the horses to be ridden on that day's Queen's would have the steam taken out of them in the Riding School. As this was a bareback exercise, it also took the steam out of the Dutymen, and resulted in many of us getting binned. Some, though fortunately never me, ended up in the medical centre. On my first Queen's, as Her Majesty was not in London, it was a Short Guard, without an officer or a Standard. I remember feeling as tall as Mount Everest as I rode out of the Ceremonial Gate for my first duty. In fact, I felt as proud as of anything that I had done, except having kids. Speaking of whom, I also remember the pride that I felt one day, while waiting to ride out of Knightsbridge for yet another Queen's, when I heard a little voice with a strong Bajan accent say: 'That's my daddy!' It was Erin, who was attending the kindergarten school in the barracks. An officer went over to find her, took her by the hand, and led her over to me. It was a magic moment that could only have happened at Knightsbridge.

The normal routine of the daily mounting of The Queen's Life Guard, involves the New Guard (drawn from one Squadron) replacing the Old Guard (formed by the other) at eleven o'clock. At this time, it had been adjusted to account for the building works at Horse Guards to create the new Household Cavalry Museum, which eventually opened in 2007. These works intruded into The Queen's Life Guard stables, temporarily reducing their capacity to the point so there wasn't room for both the Old and the New Guards' horses. To solve this problem, the blacks required for Queen's were stabled there for the duration of the building works. However, to maintain the spectacle for the public, the New Guard still rode down to take over the duties of the Old Guard; but after performing the guard change, they would then ride back to barracks, stable their horses and then drive to Horse Guards in a minibus to replace the Old Guard, who would then take the transport back to Knightsbridge. It sounds more complicated than it was.

Meanwhile, I was developing a reputation as a 'clean' soldier and was frequently given a box on Queen's. In fact, I was gaining such a reputation that I was asked if I wanted to compete for the Richmond Cup the following year. I turned it down, because I still had my sights set firmly on HCR, and didn't want to let anything get in the way of a posting to the armoured Regiment. I still dreamed of driving a Scimitar armoured car across the Canadian prairie, although I was loving my time with the horses at Knightsbridge, even when things went wrong.

Probably my worst moment came when, acting as the Stable Guard on Queen's, I was helping Trooper Waincott (now a Staff Corporal with HCR) to tack up a horse called *Zeus*. This black had a bit of a reputation, having binned Captain Harley in the Forecourt of Buckingham Palace during a State Visit, just as The Queen passed in front of the Escort. On this particular day, he was behaving really badly, bucking and rearing as we tried to get him ready for guard. Eventually, and unable to stop him, *Zeus* reared up so high on his back legs that he tumbled over backwards into a narrow stairwell. It took a crane to extricate him; he was then put in a horse ambulance and taken to the sick lines at Knightsbridge. Very sadly, he died the next day of his injuries and shock. This really upset us all.

When not coping with difficult horses, I was developing a reputation amongst the Troop Corporals of Horse for reliability and common sense. CoH Fitzgerald, who was in charge of 2 Troop, was having trouble with a lad from St Lucia, who was complaining of racism, and asked me to have a word with him. I quickly discovered that the problem had nothing to do with his colour and everything to do with a lazy attitude to work. Even then, such accusations were being used by the unscrupulous to cover their own shortcomings. I have no hesitation in stating here that during my entire time with HCMR, as at Pirbright and later with HCR, I never encountered any racial prejudice. None of the officers or NCOs (from Colonel Griffin downwards) would have tolerated it for a micro-second had it existed, which it didn't.

There were, of course, many other duties at Knightsbridge, some of which were daily. These included Watering Order, which takes place early every morning, except on Sundays when the blacks have a rest day. It involves all the horses at Knightsbridge being exercised in groups of ten to twenty around the streets of London, often with each soldier riding one horse and leading another. As a source of mishaps, Watering Order is a deep well and I have many memories of those moments, the worst of which I can recall as clearly as if it happened this morning.

Although strictly forbidden, it was common practice for Watering Order to stop for a coffee, particularly in winter. On this particular occasion, everyone except me (I don't like coffee) had dismounted to fetch their drinks from a café, when one of the horses took off. As the only person still in the saddle, I followed it in hot pursuit. Like all cavalry blacks, this one knew exactly what it was doing and led me on a helter-skelter dash, through red lights and dodging double-decker buses, in a wide right-handed circle around the streets of Shepherds Bush, returning a mile-and-a-half later, none the worse for wear, to the café from which it had bolted. The Corporal of Horse in charge of Watering Order, who will remain nameless, was relieved to say the least; I'd saved him from a pile of shit.

On another occasion, I was riding *Blenheim* and leading an excitable young horse called *Gemma*, who had only just arrived at Knightsbridge from remount training, along with a reputation for lashing out with both her front and rear hooves. When a man on a scooter got rather too close, I politely asked him to give us a bit of space. In reply, he gave me the finger. *Gemma* was not amused and left fly with a kick that sent the idiot reeling into the gutter. 'Ride, TROT!' called out the Corporal of Horse, and we swiftly left the scene. On another morning, we were riding around Soho. As we passed a terraced house in a narrow street, the lights went on in a first-floor window, and four naked ladies flashed. It could only happen on Watering Order . . . and it frequently did.

Other duties at Knightsbridge were less stimulating, although no less exciting – and one of the first of these I also found very moving. Every November the Royal British Legion holds the Festival of Remembrance at the Royal Albert Hall on the eve of Remembrance Sunday. One of the highlights of this event at that time was when veterans, many of them disabled, march down the aisles to join the servicemen on the floor of the hall. On this particular evening, I was on duty in dismounted Full Dress, tasked with escorting a double-below-the-knee amputee into the arena. As we waited, he told me of his experiences in Belgium in 1940, during the retreat to Dunkirk. I have thought a lot since then about what he said: the loss of many friends he had grown up with, worked with and trained with; and the sheer bloody awfulness of the conditions in which he had fought. I later reflected on our conversation, when I was in Afghanistan. Without playing down our situation there, we had it easy by comparison with what he had gone through.

Less harrowing, but nonetheless emotionally moving duties at Knights-bridge included Mounted Escorts for State Visits. My first such duty was for the visit of the President of Ghana in March 2007. Those who haven't served at Knightsbridge probably think that on the first day of a State Visit, the Escort simply forms up in the yard at Knightsbridge, rides to Bucking-ham Palace, from where it escorts Her Majesty to Horse Guards Parade, waits for the arrival of the Visitor, and then escorts The Queen's carriage back up The Mall before returning to barracks. If only it were that simple. For a start – in additions to the hours of kit cleaning – there were the Early Morning Rehearsals, which are carried out while London sleeps and the streets are free of traffic. With Stables at 1 a.m., followed by Mount Up at 2 a.m. in order to be at Buckingham Palace by 3 a.m., such duties are bloody hard work for all concerned. The same happens for The Queen's Birthday Parade (Trooping the Colour) and the annual State Opening of Parliament. But for me, it was all worth it. After all, I was the first black Bajan ever to ride on Trooping or an Escort.

As I sat on *Albert* on that March morning on Horse Guards Parade, facing the dais where Her Majesty was waiting for the arrival of the President of Ghana, the Foot Guards band struck up the National Anthem and tears started rolling down my cheeks. Who would have thought, at that moment, that the little boy from Saint John, Barbados, would end up on a horse in front of The Queen of Barbados and the United Kingdom? 'How was that for you?' I was asked by a guy, who was handing out bottles of chilled beer for all the dutymen when we eventually got back to Knightsbridge. 'Pretty awesome,' I replied, before taking a swig while leading *Albert* down the ramp into The Life Guards' stables – and I meant it.

I won't even canter you through the rest of the range of public duties that I carried out while at HCMR (all of which are covered in detail in my co-author's illustrated book, *Uniquely British: A Year in the Life of the Household Cavalry*). For me they included more State Visits, a State Opening of Parliament, the Lord Mayor's Show and various staircase-lining duties at the Palace of Westminster and Buckingham Palace, during one of which The Queen stopped to talk to me. However, like the late Captain Sir Tom Moore, I am not going to repeat it here. For some reason, although I was on it, I don't recall much of the Household Cavalry Pageant, held on Horse Guards Parade in June 2007 to mark the opening of the Household Cavalry Museum by The Queen. This doesn't make my co-author very happy as he devised, wrote, produced and directed the Pageant. As I told him, that year was so damned busy that it's all now a bit of a blur.

Before running down the curtain on my time with HCMR, there are a couple more things that I would like to record. The first was the very real pleasure that I got when, while in a box on Queen's, Marketha and my mum turned up unannounced in front of me; and then there were those times when the girls would come and watch me during guard change. Once, Marketha turned up at Horse Guards in her night clothes having locked herself out of the flat. That was both embarrassing and funny, although not nearly as embarrassing or funny as the activities of some of the tourists with the box men, but I'll draw a veil over that.

Considerably less funny was the time when I was on duty in a box, and noticed some men in a car who seemed to be taking an unusual interest in the Horse Guards building and Queen's. It was probably my training in the police that made me watch them. While the car circled, a couple got out and seemed to recce the yard and the arch. There is an alarm bell inside each of the boxes and I pressed mine. The Guard Corporal of Horse immediately joined me from his desk in the Guard Room and I told him of my suspicions. Later, Garrison Sergeant Major Billy Mott came down from his office in the Horse Guards building and congratulated me on being alert. 'People think that we are here for show,' he said, 'but – as you have just proved – we are really here to guard Her Majesty. Well done, Mapp.'

Towards the end of 2007, I was sent on a course to learn how to drive a tracked armoured vehicle (CVR(T)) with which HCR was equipped. Yes, Knightsbridge was great, I really loved the horses, and I had been approached to join the Riding Staff with a promise of promotion. But I was not to be deflected from my goal of driving a Scimitar.

CHAPTER 6

Marilyn Monroe

IN MID-MARCH 2008, I arrived at Combermere Barracks in Windsor and joined 'A' Squadron of the Household Cavalry Regiment (HCR). I moved Marketha and our two girls into married quarters (accommodation) in Windsor, from where she commuted to her job in London. I had loved my time at Knightsbridge, but this was where I had always wanted to be, as a part of the Household Cavalry's operational fighting unit, elements of which had been on active service almost continuously since 1945.

The public only sees the ceremonial side of our Regiments, but the gallantry and medal ribbons worn on my mates' tunics told a different story. Indeed, I would be serving with one of the Army's most highly decorated soldiers, Corporal of Horse (later Regimental Corporal Major) Mick Flynn, who had been awarded the Conspicuous Gallantry Cross (CGC) for an action in Iraq in 2003 and the Military Cross (MC) for one in Afghanistan in 2006. Known affectionately as the 'Bullet Magnet', I was told soon after I arrived: 'Don't ever stand next to Mick, it's too bloody dangerous.'

Until May 2019, when HCR moved to Bulford Camp in Wiltshire so that it could be re-equipped with the new Ajax armoured fighting vehicle, Combermere had been the UK home of the Household Cavalry's operational unit since the end of the Second World War, and a Household Cavalry barracks since the eighteenth century. Unlike at Knightsbridge, where The Life Guards and The Blues and Royals each had a Squadron, at Combermere the two cap badges were mixed up between four Squadrons, although inter-regimental rivalries going back generations still existed.

After two very enjoyable years of soldiering on horses, I was more than ready to be a front-line soldier. However, at first the regime at HCR came as something of a shock. Instead of having to work every hour of the day, looking after horses, and cleaning kit for The Queen's Life Guard and other public duties, with only one thirty-six-hour leave pass every two weeks, life at Windsor was comparatively easy. I had arrived expecting to be run ragged, only to find that it was all rather relaxed. After morning PT (physical training), we would go to the vehicle park, where there were no wagons on which to work when I first arrived.

This idleness was not to last, and soon 'A' Squadron was deployed to act as enemy on a training exercise with one of our other Squadrons, who were preparing to be deployed in Afghanistan. I had a great time, running around dressed in a dish-dash as a Taliban fighter, armed with an AK-47 rifle, and I felt a real sense of pride and awe when the legendary Mick Flynn drove past me in his Scimitar, the heaviest-armed vehicle in the CVR(T) family. We went on several other exercises, during which we assisted the Parachute Regiment with their pre-Afghanistan training.

Then it was time to go to Castlemartin Camp in Pembrokeshire for live gunnery training on the ranges there. As I had been trained as a CVR(T) driver while at Knightsbridge, I didn't get to fire the Scimitar's 30 mm RARDEN cannon on this occasion. However, we did several March & Shoot exercises, in which we 'tabbed' (a tactical advance to battle) in full kit from the camp to the ranges, where we fired our rifles using live ammunition. Other live-firing training included practicing basic infantry skills, like Section attacks. Back once again in Windsor, I was put on a series of training courses to teach me radio and gunnery, the other two basic skills of a CVR(T) soldier. Although I found learning to operate a Bowman radio interesting, I soon realised that life as a radio operator was quite boring. It also carried with it the opportunity to make a fool of yourself on the net.

Gunnery was something else. In fact, once I started to learn about it, it blew my mind. All training can be dull, even if you are interested in the subject; but when it is taught by someone like Corporal of Horse Byron Gibson, who was my instructor, it can also be great fun. Our gunnery training took place in the classroom at Windsor and then on the range at the AFV Gunnery School at Lulworth Camp in Dorset. We learned to maintain, operate and fire the Scimitar's RARDEN cannon as well as its co-axially mounted 7.62 mm General Purpose Machine Gun (GPMG or 'co-ax'). The Army loves to use mnemonics and catch phrases in its skills teaching, and one particular GPMG gunnery drill was no exception: 'The way to remember the length of time to hold the trigger when using the co-ax,' said Byron Gibson, 'is to squeeze it only for as long as it takes to say, Marilyn Monroe...Marilyn Monroe...Marilyn Monroe had big tits.' No one was going to forget that in a hurry.

Out on the ranges, overlooking a beautiful cove and surrounded by wonderful scenery, we were able to fire the Scimitar's guns, with the RARDEN cannon loaded with 30 mm HE (high explosive) shells. These made very satisfying explosions when they hit the targets, which trundled across in front our wagons. But the sight of our 30 mm shells hitting a target was nothing like as awesome as the sound from the next-door range where Challenger 2 tanks were firing their 120 mm main armament. You would definitely not want to be on the receiving end of that.

By the beginning of June 2008, I was back at Windsor and working on maintaining my vehicle. With the rest of 'A' Squadron I also helped 'D' Squadron prepare for yet another tour in Afghanistan. Around this time, I was moved as a driver to my Squadron's Support Troop, where I worked with a bunch of guys who had seen active service on Operation TELIC 10 (June-December 2007) in Iraq. My new vehicle commander was Lance Corporal of Horse Andrew Phelan, always cool and completely relaxed, but dead professional. Andy made me feel as though I'd always been a member of my new Troop and became an important person in this story.

While at Windsor, my Squadron Leader had been happy to give me time to try-out for the Army volleyball team. The Regiment liked being repres-ented in Army sport, and supported me when I won a place in the team.

This was largely made up of Fijians and men from Africa, many of whom were serving in the Army Air Corps or the Adjutant General's Corps. I later met some of these guys in Afghanistan, and later still at Headley Court, the Defence Medical Rehabilitation Centre. We did pretty well and finished that year as runners-up to the RAF in the inter-services competition.

However, not everything was going well at this time. Possibly because of the volleyball I was playing, or it may have been because of PT, the injury that I had suffered in the Barbados Defence Force Reserves, and which had given me trouble in Basic Training, flared up again. As at Pirbright, this caused real pain in my left hip and up the left side of my back. Sometimes I couldn't complete a run, and if I did, I would be left completely numb in my back. For some reason, pride probably, I didn't report it, which led to some people thinking that I was shirking on PT. Looking back, not going to the see the medics was a pretty stupid thing to do.

Towards the end of July, half of the Squadron, including Support Troop, prepared to go to the British Army Training Unit Suffield (BATUS), Canada, where we were to provide the enemy on training exercises for five months. As I drew my desert combat kit from the QM's stores, I started to feel like a real soldier for the first time.

BATUS is located in Alberta, on the Canadian Forces Base (CFB) in the vast prairie that stretches for hundreds of miles eastwards from the Rockies. At twenty per cent of the size of Northern Ireland, the CFB is the British Army's largest training area. Uninhabited by anything except gophers and rattlesnakes, it allows armoured formations to train using live ammunition and 'tactical effect simulation'. The camp itself is large, the nearest civilisation is a one-horse 'city' called Medicine Hat (about half-an-hour's drive from the camp) and the nearest real city is Calgary, some 155 miles away to the west.

To get there we flew to Calgary on an elderly RAF TriStar transport aeroplane from RAF Brize Norton in Oxfordshire. Having always wanted to be a pilot, I have no fear of flying. But when our TriStar took off, I damn nearly shat myself; the noise and the smell of fuel was awful. I was sitting next to my really good mate, Jordan 'Dinger' Bell, who was my closest friend in the Squadron, my neighbour on the 'patch' (married quarters) back in Windsor, and later became my third daughter's godfather. 'We're going to die here,' I murmured to him, at which he gave me a wry smile.

At last, we landed at Calgary, where we were welcomed by the Canadians with the red-carpet treatment, and then we piled onto buses for the three-hour drive to BATUS. I had been expecting a tented camp. Instead, we were shown into accommodation blocks equipped with telephone, WiFi, and a restaurant that served great American breakfasts. Once we'd settled in, we went down to the tank park where we found a collection of very old and rather worn CVR(T)s. My wagon was a Spartan, which is the armoured personnel carrier version of the family. I could tell from the state it was in that it was going to be high maintenance.

Soon we were on our first ten-day exercise on the prairie with me in the driver's seat of the Spartan. The rest of my crew was made up of Andy Phelan in the commander's small turret with Daniel Chaplin, and Dinger inside on the radio. As we drove out of camp and onto the training area, I was completely amazed at the sheer vastness of the Canadian prairie, with nothing but rolling, treeless scrubland stretching to the far horizon.

During the day, the distances were so great and the air so clear that we could see weather fronts moving in. On one occasion we were in an OP (Observation Post) on the top of a piece of rising ground. The weather was hot and sunny, and we had concealed our wagon in a hide below the OP, from where we had run up the slope to get into position. We were ten minutes into a three-hour stag (sentry duty), when we heard on our combat radio that a wet weather front was moving in. Within a few minutes we could see it coming towards us, and soon after that we were drenched with heavy rain and pelted with hail stones. The only thing we could do was to huddle together for protection, as we had left our wet weather kit on the Spartan. Thirty minutes later it was sunny again, but we were soaked through. So we just laughed, while watching Challenger tanks in the distance, as a training battle developed.

At the end of every day, we stayed out on the prairie. If there were no night manoeuvres, we went into a leaguer (a military vehicle camp in the field). Having erected a bivvy (a simple tent attached to the side of the vehicle), we would have a wash, and then cook the evening meal from our ration packs. On the prairie there is no light pollution, so the sky at night is breath-taking; some nights we could even see the Northern Lights in the distance. When we were in these night leaguers, there would be no stag and we didn't have to monitor the radios, so Andy, Dinger, Daniel and I would just sit out under the stars and talk.

On other nights we would be driving across the prairie in our wagons, and once we came close to disaster. From my position in the driver's seat, particularly when driving closed down (with my hatch shut and only a periscope for vision), I couldn't see much. Daniel was in the turret with Andy, and Dinger was in the back of the vehicle where he could see nothing at all. So as the vehicle commander, it was Andy's job to give me directions over the intercom, from his position in the turret above and behind me, and with the benefit of his night vision goggles. We had been in contact with a Challenger tank on the opposing side, had managed to evade it, and were driving away from trouble when suddenly Andy yelled: 'STOP!' I jammed on the brakes but, as I was closed down, I couldn't see why he had given such an urgent order. I opened the hatch and looked out. We were barely inches from the edge of a large canyon and immediately in front of us was a precipice. All I could think was: 'Holy shit...' My co-author told me that before his first military parachute drop, his instructor told those about to jump: 'Gentlemen, only your laundry lady will know exactly how scared you were.' That cliff edge was definitely a 'laundry lady' moment.

Even on exercise in daylight, things mostly happen at a snail's pace until you are attacked. Then things move very fast indeed. While we were out on the prairie, Andy taught me the craft of how to drive under combat conditions, by being super alert to my surroundings and using dead ground for cover. When leaguered up, I also had to ensure that, as far as possible, my wagon was in good running order. This was good advice, as the training area was littered with deep, concealed tank ditches, which had to be avoided at all costs by vehicles like mine. There were also times when we needed to hide, and moments when we needed to be sure we could escape at maximum speed.

One day on that first exercise, we were providing a screen (outer defensive ring) for an infantry formation as it cleared through a village. I watched it from our concealed position in dead ground, parked up side-on behind the crest of a rise, on the side away from the advancing enemy Challenger tanks. The infantrymen were doing a brilliant job demonstrating why the British Army is the best in the world. Andy and Daniel were in the turret, and Dinger was inside the vehicle, probably on the radio. Fortunately, as always, I had one earpiece of my intercom and radio headset slightly away from my ear. Without any warning, I suddenly heard the roar of a Challenger tank engine at the same time as Andy. Looking up at the crest, we both saw the underside of a tank and its tracks, just as it was about to pitch down the slope and land on top of us. Andy yelled: 'Move! Move!' The Challenger's sixty-three tons of armoured steel would have squashed us flat and its driver would have seen us only when it was too late. Thank God it wasn't travelling fast and I managed to drive out of its way, but it had been a very close shave. Once we had recovered from the shock, we once again had a good laugh. Well, what else could we do?

Because all our vehicles were rather elderly, on the rough terrain of the prairie they were constantly throwing tracks or breaking torsion bars, which are an essential component of the vehicle's drive train. From necessity, I quickly became an expert at making running repairs in the field. Eventually, the first exercise ended and we returned to camp, to find that more men had flown in from Windsor. After rolling back the wagons (post-exercise vehicle maintenance), I had a shower and a good sleep.

The following day, Dinger and I headed into Medicine Hat. The choice of entertainment there was strictly limited, and Montana's BBQ & Bar was about the only place to eat and drink. Inevitably, we had to mix with the local cowboys, who were much less welcoming than the Canadian military. Although Dinger and I kept ourselves to ourselves, other lads in the Squadron had run-ins with them, usually when a girl was involved. My opportunities for getting into trouble were, however, limited as I had signed up to spend most of our first five-day R&R (Rest and Recuperation) adventure training.

This took place at Trail's End Camp in the foothills of the Rockies. We were driven there in a bus and, once we'd arrived, we were given a choice of adventures. As a former pony soldier, I decided to go on a horse trail in the mountains. It was a good decision as the experience was fantastic. One night we camped-out half-way up a peak and had a barbecue. Then afterwards our cowboy guides showed us how to fire their rifles at tin cans on poles. It was stuff straight out of a western. The next morning, we left the horses in camp, trekked on foot to the top of the mountain, took some photos, clambered back down, and rode back to base camp.

On my return to BATUS, the first thing I heard was that HRH Prince Harry, known to us as 'Captain Wales', had been appointed second-in-command of 'A' Squadron and would be joining us for the second exercise. I had never met him, and when I did, I found him to be very friendly and more than happy to be one of us. He had recently returned from his first tour in Afghanistan on Operation HERRICK 7 (November 2007–April 2008: Operation HERRICK was the codename for all British operation in Afghanistan 2002–2014).

That first meeting happened pretty quickly because, no sooner was I back in camp, than Dinger messaged me saying that I should join him in Medicine Hat for dinner. At Montana's, I was sitting at the bar with Dinger and a couple of lads, when Prince Harry came over to join us with his Personal Protection Officer. With the Prince egging us on, we managed to convince the waitresses that one of our officers, who was sitting having dinner at a table on the other side of the room, was actually Captain Wales. Within in a minute, all Montana's waitresses had crowded around the officers' table. We all, Prince Harry included, cracked-up.

That was the good news. The bad news for me was that Andy Phelan had been recalled to Windsor, and I was also to be separated from Dinger, as I had been selected to drive either Prince Harry or our Squadron Leader in the next exercise. The choice was not down to me and, because he knew of my night driving skills, the Squadron Leader decided to make me his driver. This initially boosted my confidence, but later led to trouble. Our wagon was a clapped-out old Salamander, a modified Scorpion light tank used only at BATUS. On the first day that I drove it in camp, the bloody vehicle not only refused to go at anything but a snail's pace, but also broke down and continued to do so, no matter how much work I or the Squadron's REME LAD (Royal Electrical & Mechanical Engineers Light Aid Detachment) did on it.

Almost from the start, I was sure there was a problem with the fuel supply system, but all the experts disagreed with me. By the time I had stripped down and bled the whole system on my own initiative, and cured the problem, it was too late. For not only was the Salamander slow and unreliable, which pissed off my boss, but we also had a series of mishaps.

First, when urged by him to go faster, I narrowly avoided colliding with a large boulder on the prairie, concealed in a clump of tall grass. If I had hit it, I would have been badly injured and might have broken my neck. This near miss was bad enough, but it was followed by a drive from one leaguer to another, during which he told me simply to follow the Royal Tank Regiment who were in the lead. Because of the dust thrown up by their tank tracks, I had to drive really slowly. This infuriated him, and he gave me yet another bollocking over the intercom.

Getting out of the Salamander at the end of the drive, I felt broken. Prince Harry was standing nearby, and as my Squadron Leader stomped off, I asked the Prince if I could have a word with him. When he said yes, I told him that I was really struggling. 'You are driving for one of the hardest people in the Regiment,' Prince Harry replied, 'and you must bear in mind who he is. But keep your head up. You'll be OK.' A short time later, I was able to apologise to my Squadron Leader, who told me not to worry about it. But when we drove back to camp at the end of the exercise, I was still not driving fast enough for him, we had more words, and he told me to pull over. As Prince Harry passed us, my boss yelled at him to take over leading the column to BATUS. By the time I got to my room, my confidence was completely shattered. I didn't socialise with the lads; instead, I took advantage of a Commonwealth-sponsored return airline ticket to Barbados, and flew off to spend the five-days of R&R with my family.

When my leave was over, I got back to BATUS to find that Prince Harry had returned to Windsor, my Squadron Leader had taken HRH's driver, and I had been assigned to a recently arrived officer for the next exercise. It went well, but I knew in my heart that, despite some reassurances from my Squadron Leader, he no longer rated me. As proof of this, while waiting at Calgary airport for our flight back to the UK, I found myself sitting opposite him. 'Mind my bag for me, would you?' asked Dinger, who was sitting next to me and wanted to take a leak. During the time he was away, I think I may have dozed off. Anyway, no sooner had Dinger returned than my Squadron Leader got up, and rather pointedly asked Dinger – not me – to keep an eye on his bag, as he too went to ease-springs. It was obvious to me that I had fallen from grace.

Looking back on that time in Canada, I now realise that other pressures may have been partly responsible for my difficulties; Marketha was pregnant with our third child, and it bothered me that I was away when I should have been at home. Trying to deal at long distance with these things, as well as coping with the military issues just described, was not easy. In fact, when I got back to Windsor, I found that everything at home was fine and Marketha was coping well, helped by Sissy who had flown over to be with her for the birth.

I used the short post-BATUS leave period to reconnect with my family, but only a week later the Squadron was back at Castlemartin for more gunnery training. As before, I didn't get to sit in the gunner's seat; but I did undertake a lot more infantry skills training, which I would need when the Squadron went to Afghanistan. This was followed by some much-needed Christmas leave.

. . .

On my return to barracks early in the New Year, I was sent for by 'A' Squadron Leader who told me that as I was, in his words, 'a family man', the Squadron was not for me and he was transferring me to Headquarters Squadron to work in the Regimental Quartermaster's stores. If I was disappointed at being pulled out of the front line, I didn't have time to dwell on it, for almost immediately Marketha went into premature labour and it was soon clear that the birth would be by C-section. Although I'd been born that way, I found this a very distressing experience. Watching Marketha in pain was agonising. When my new daughter Alexa appeared, she was tiny – not much bigger than my outstretched hand – and had to spend several weeks in an incubator. Thank God, my mum had flown over to be with us, as no sooner had I welcomed Alexa into the world on 6th January 2009, than I had to deploy with Regimental Headquarters for an exercise on Salisbury Plain in Wiltshire.

Actually, dealing with the issues at home was much easier from my job in the QM's stores than it would have been if I had stayed with 'A' Squadron. So with hindsight, I'm now really grateful to my former Squadron Leader for his decision to move me on. I was also fortunate that the lads in the stores were a great bunch, and I learned a lot about the admin side of life in an armoured reconnaissance Regiment. This was all stuff that I had previously taken for granted. Not only that, but with all the Sabre Squadrons (front line units) deployed away from Windsor, the barracks was really quiet in those early months of 2009.

This gave me an opportunity not only to help out at home, but also to get a grip of the old groin injury that had given me so much pain the previous year. Untreated, the injury would have prevented me from passing a Combat Fitness Test (CFT), which I would need if I was to return to front line duties, as I privately planned. So, I reported to the Medical Officer, gave up volleyball, and was sent on a rehabilitation course in Aldershot which sorted out the problem.

In the spring, while still working in the stores, I was told that I was to be sent on a Mastiff driver's course. Mastiff is a heavily armoured, six-wheeled protected patrol vehicle, with a V-shaped hull or underside to deflect IEDs, that the Army had acquired for use in Afghanistan. With my groin injury sorted, my CFT passed, and by doing this course there was now no reason why I should not return to a Sabre Squadron and, in due course, be deployed on Operation HERRICK in Afghanistan.

However, although we hadn't discussed it, I knew that going back to one of the Sabre Squadrons was not something that Marketha wanted me to do. At the same time, I was being encouraged to stay with the QM stores: 'You are doing well,' said my immediate boss in the stores, Corporal of Horse Anthony Pettipher, 'and you could make a career here. I know you want to go to Afghanistan, but sooner or later Headquarters Squadron *will* be deployed to Camp Bastion, so you'll get to go there...' But I knew in my heart that I had not joined the British Army to sit in the QM's stores, while my mates were fighting the Taliban. I decided to leave the decision to Fate, who duly came knocking with the news that I was being transferred to 'C' Squadron, which was to be deployed on Operation HERRICK 11 (November 2009–April 2010).

When I reported to the Squadron's office, I was told that I would be a driver with 3 Troop, which would be equipped in Afghanistan with Mastiffs, although we were later to get Scimitars as well. Under the command of Lieutenant Barnabas Campbell, the Troop's 'three-bar' (the rank insignia of a Corporal of Horse is three chevrons surmounted by a crown) was Corporal of Horse Matthew 'Jerry' McGuire. From the get go, Jerry made me feel at home: 'I'm not interested in what happened to you in 'A' Squadron,' he said, '*we* are really pleased to have you on board for Afghan. All that I require of you is to be in the right place at the right time – and *never* shave with your shirt on.' This was just one of Jerry's rules or values; he was a very easy-going guy with lots of humour, but he'd been an instructor at Pirbright, which may account for those quirks of his.

The Squadron was due to fly out to Afghanistan in September, but before then we went yet again to Castlemartin where, this time, I at last got to fire the RARDEN cannon on the range. That was epic. There was also a lot of pre-deployment training that was specific to our upcoming duty. This included training with a Vallon metal detector, which we would use for four-man Op BARMA IED clearance operations, and special radio procedures including the '9-liner' (medical evacuation request) to be used in the case of a casualty. Then there was a final exercise before we had to pack-up our kit for deployment. For some reason, Trooper Oliver 'Oli' Williams (who I'd served with in 'A' Squadron) and I were not to travel out to Afghanistan with the rest of 'C' Squadron, but to follow on a few days later.

Although I joined the Army to serve on the front line, the reality of that was at last coming home to both me and Marketha. The TV news announced injuries and deaths in Afghanistan on an almost daily basis, and it was clearly no computer war game. I know that Marketha was very worried, although she tried not to show it, and I know that we both remembered the dream of many years before, which predicted my dad's death and forecast my own. On top of this, she was coping with a new baby as well as our two older girls; I had the additional worries that the money I was sending to my family in Barbados was putting a massive strain on our finances; and my mum had just had surgery for breast cancer. It was not a good time to be going off to war.

At last, the day of departure dawned – actually, I had to get going at 2 a.m., so the late-September dawn was a way off – and a taxi to take me into barracks arrived. I stood in my sitting room and looked at my wife and my girls. I wasn't afraid of what was to come, but I was scared about what would happen to my family if I didn't return. 'What am I doing?' I thought. 'Why have I chosen to leave Marketha and the girls? Will I ever see them again?' I have no shame in telling you that, at that moment, the tears rolled down my cheeks. Then I pulled myself together. 'This is what I signed-up for,' I told myself. 'This is why I left Barbados and came to the UK. OK. So, get on with it.' I hugged them all and told them that I loved them. 'Don't worry about us,' said Marketha, 'we'll be fine. I'll send you lots of 'blueys' (Forces Airletters), and the other mums on the patch are there if I need them.' I left the house and got into the cab, but before it pulled away, I broke down again. The taxi driver tried to comfort me. 'You're going to be fine,' he said, as he patted me on the shoulder, 'and thank you for what you are doing.' I manned-up at that.

Once at Combermere, I made my way to the Squadron office, where Oli Williams was waiting for me. At that moment, I don't know how or why, I went into a different space in my head, switched-off from my domestic life and switched-on military mode. A short time later a minibus took us to RAF Brize Norton where, as usual, we waited … and waited … and I fretted about the prospect of another white-knuckle ride on a crap TriStar. Eventually, we were loaded onto an aeroplane but, miracle of miracles, it was not a TriStar, but a normal civvy-style airliner which flew us in comfort to the Al Minhad Air Base, south of Dubai. As we took off from Brize Norton, I looked out of the window and was struck by the beauty of what I was leaving behind. Years previously at Knightsbridge I'd had a talk with a three-bar there about his experience of returning from Iraq. 'You know,' he said, 'the most striking thing when you come back is the beauty of the English countryside.' He was right; but I was not coming home, I was leaving, and so I tried to fix England's green fields in my mind.

When we got off the aircraft at Al Minhad several hours later, the green fields of England had been replaced by the sand, heat and humidity of the Middle East, all of which hit me like a brick wall. Al Minhad was not, however, our destination that day and we later transferred to an RAF Boeing C-17 Globemaster that was to fly us under cover of darkness to Camp Bastion, the main military airbase in Afghanistan. The contrast in aeroplane interiors could not have been greater, for the C-17 was a no-frills military transport aircraft, with seating along the fuselage and piles of kit strapped down the middle. Before take-off, the RAF captain spoke to us on the intercom: 'This is going to be rough, particularly the approach to Camp Bastion, so brace yourselves.'

In the event, all went smoothly until we were approaching our destination. We were ordered to put on our helmets and the cabin lights were doused. The C-17 then started making a series of very steep turns, while firing flares as a precaution against enemy missiles. It was a horrible experience, even for someone like me who loved flying. The G-force (gravitational pull) of the turns was considerable, and some of the lads started puking. I wasn't scared, but I was damn glad when the aircraft landed with a squeal of brakes, followed by a very abrupt halt. Almost immediate the tail ramp was lowered, Oli and I grabbed our bags and stepped down onto the tarmac of Camp Bastion airfield. We had arrived – but what lay in wait for us?

CHAPTER 7

Mount Doom

BRITISH TROOPS HAD BEEN deployed in Afghanistan since 2002, as part of the NATO-led International Security Assistance Force (ISAF). They were tasked with supporting the legitimate government of Afghanistan, first with military training, and then by driving out the Taliban insurgents. Units of the Household Cavalry Regiment had been part of ISAF in 2006 (Operation HERRICK 4), and again in 2007-2008 (Operation HERRICK 7 and 8). In 2009-10 (Operation HERRICK 11) RHQ, 'C' Squadron and elements of 'A' Squadron were deployed. The British area of operation was Helmand Province, in the south of the country. This was the most lawless and dangerous zone of operations, with the Taliban committed to forcing us out through constant small-scale attacks and the widespread use of concealed improvised explosive devices (IEDs). Our base for the tour in Helmand was the District Centre, a town called Musa Qala, which had been the scene of very heavy fighting in previous years. But first we had to get there.

Although it was still dark when we arrived at Camp Bastion, I could see that it was huge: a proper little city in the middle of nowhere. We went from the aeroplane to a regimental RV (rendezvous), where we were met by Corporal of Horse John Brophy, and then driven in a Land Rover to our tented accommodation. I thanked God when I realised that it was air-conditioned. After breakfast the following morning, we were given a RSOI (Reception, Staging, Onward Movement and Integration) briefing which covered a description of the camp, details of what was happening 'in theatre' and what we would be doing for the next couple of days. This included acclimatisation, drawing new Osprey body armour and upgraded protective helmets from the stores, and being issued with new personal weapons fitted with the latest ACOG sights (Advanced Combat Optical Gunsight). These weapons had to be 'zeroed' (adjusting the sight to the weapon), which took place on a firing range outside the camp perimeter. As the Taliban had previously placed IEDs on the ranges, which had killed some guys, we went there on a real tactical patrol, surrounded by force protection vehicles: 'Wow,' I thought, 'I really am a million miles from home.'

Later we were given briefings on how the Taliban were operating, and some more training on a new version of the Vallon metal detector. It really struck me at this time that every bit of equipment we were going to use in Helmand was the very latest, in stark contrast to the kit we had back in the UK. We also explored the camp. The US lines had a fantastic canteen, which served every kind of food you can imagine. Their fridges were a treasure trove of goodness and we raided them as often as we could. Fortunately, the Yanks liked the food in our canteen and did the same to our supplies.

On the morning of the second day that I was in Camp Bastion, I was woken by a tremendously loud alarm. I quickly found out that this signalled Operation MINIMISE, an operational procedure which suspends all non-official external communications. It was activated whenever there was a major casualty or a fatality, so that the family of the dead or injured soldier could be informed by the military authorities, rather than hearing it from a mate using a mobile or a satellite phone. That was a real eye-opener, but it was not my last reality check at Camp Bastion.

On the third or it may have been the fourth day, we heard that there was to be a repatriation parade for a paratrooper who had been killed in action. Back home in England, like everyone else, I had seen on the TV news coffins being unloaded with great ceremony at RAF Brize Norton, and then being driven away for burial through the village of Wootton Bassett (now Royal Wootton Bassett), where the locals turned out every time to pay their respects. I had never seen footage of the ceremony at Camp Bastion. The entire garrison paraded on the airfield tarmac and stood in a horseshoe

ABOVE LEFT
Dad, Mum and me on my wedding day,
21st December 2002

ABOVE
Me and Dad in the church at my wedding

LEFT
Marketha and me on our wedding day

BELOW
Royal Barbados Police Force Canine Unit
graduation, 2003

ABOVE
Reece Foran and me at the
Household Cavalry Mounted
Regiment Kit Ride Pass Off,
2006

LEFT
On duty on The Queen's Life
Guard, Whitehall, London,
2007

At Montana's, Medicine Hat, with some of the lads and Captain Wales, 2008, me on the far right

At BATUS with Andy Phelan and Daniel Chaplin, 2008

ABOVE
The Army Volleyball Team,
2008

LEFT
The day I left for Afghanistan,
October 2009

On patrol in Helmand Province, Afghanistan, with an Op Barma team in front of Titanium 33, 2009

On a firing range at Camp Bastion, Afghanistan, October 2009

LEFT
Driving Titanium 33 on patrol, November 2009

BELOW
On my Scimitar, Titanium 33, December 2009

TOP
Christmas 2009 in Afghanistan

ABOVE
Me taking cover under Titanium 33 during a Taliban mortar attack, January 2010

OPPOSITE
Titanium 33 after the IED incident on 31st January 2010

TOP
My daughters Jodie, Alexa and Erin in January 2010

ABOVE
At an HIV hostel, Uganda, 2010

Reception at the British High Commission, Bridgetown, Barbados: Corporal of Horse Paul 'Doc' Holiday, me, Corporal of Horse Matthew 'Jerry' McGuire, Christmas 2010

The UK Armed Forces 4 × 100 m Relay Team, Warrior Games 2014, Colorado Springs, USA: Me, Kushal Limbu, Dave Henson and Matt Webb

Photo: Viestur

ABOVE
2018 World Cup winner, St Moritz,
Switzerland

ABOVE RIGHT
Overall World Cup champion, 2018,
with Christopher Stewart and Lonnie
Bissonette

RIGHT
Rupert Fryer and me, St Moritz,
Switzerland, 2019, with World Cup
trophy

Lonnie Bissonette and me,
Lillehammer, Norway, 2019

After winning the 2nd race in
Lillehammer, 2019

Winning Silver in the World
Championship, 2019, at Lake
Placid, USA

The winning run for the
European Championship at
Oberhof, Germany, in 2020
with Sarah Monk

At work with the Wilshire Police, 2020

formation around the tailgate of a C-130 Hercules aircraft, in front of which lay the body in its Union flag-draped coffin.

A religious service followed, during which the paratrooper's friends spoke in a way that was incredibly moving, but must have been very difficult for them; I thought it was the ultimate act of reverence and respect for a fallen comrade; and there was no shame in the tears that were on most cheeks, including mine. The coffin was then loaded into the aeroplane, which soon after took off, dipping its wings in respect once it was airborne. 'Oh, my God, I don't want that,' I thought, as images of Marketha, the girls, and everyone back at home filled my mind. I headed straight for the telephone; I simply had to be in contact with them. That night I hardly slept, as the reality of the job I was in Afghanistan to do sank in. I was definitely not at home anymore.

Not long after we arrived at Camp Bastion, Oli and I were ordered to report for additional Mastiff driver training. We already knew that we were to drive two new Mastiffs from Camp Bastion to Musa Qala and this training was to give us, and the other lads, the experience of driving on the terrain that we would be facing. It took place on a very bumpy course, during which we sat in the back of the Mastiff until it was our turn to drive. It was then that I realised for the first time that I was prone to motion sickness. Back in the tent later that day, we heard that Staff Corporal 'Paddy' Ireland and Sergeant Nathan Hunt of the Royal Engineers, both in 'C' Squadron, were due in on a Chinook (heavy-lift, twin-rotor helicopter) from Musa Qala.

The next morning Nathan and Paddy, whom I would be driving, rocked up, and we all went down to the vehicle park to prepare our new Mastiffs and then load our kit for the drive to Musa Qala. As well as getting these new vehicles to 'C' Squadron, we were also part of the force protection for a large re-supply convoy which included Gurkhas and Royal Marines. With Apache attack helicopters flying overhead, this convoy was to drive non-stop for twenty-six hours to Musa Qala, via Forward Operating Base (FOB) Edinburgh.

The move-out from Camp Bastion was scheduled for a minute after midnight that night, but before then we had to form up the convoy and – as usual – sit and wait. By the time we did move, I was nearly screaming, 'Let's get going!' That drive was what I can only describe as a very heightened experience. I had never driven for that long before without a break, and I think I survived off adrenalin. After the first couple of miles, we were on un-made roads, and the convoy was not without its dramas. Although we didn't come under attack, the Gurkhas who were map-reading had problems and the terrain was incredibly rough. It was a real test for the Mastiff, but with Paddy giving me some much-needed reassurance, we made it to a wadi just short of the Battle Group's FOB Edinburgh, the resupply point for our base in Musa Qala.

There we were met by CoH Jerry McGuire, who with 'C' Squadron was marking the route to the FOB. he told me that in future I would be driving for Lance Corporal of Horse Ruel 'Frankie' Francis. Although I really wanted to be the gunner, the other member of our crew was Scott 'Scotty' Porter, who was senior to me and so got to handle the o.50-inch Browning Machine Gun mounted in the turret on the roof of the Mastiff. Oli would be going to 5 Troop to drive for Paddy Ireland, who was the Troop Leader. At FOB Edinburgh, we were deep into Taliban territory and the risk of hitting IEDs on the rest of the route was much increased. We all regarded the Mastiffs as safe against IED, whereas the aluminium armoured Scimitars, which I would drive in the future, were very vulnerable. Under the command of Major Justin Butah, 'C' Squadron was designated a Mastiff group, but 3 Troop had a dual-role and would, once they were issued, also have CVR(T)s.

On our way to Musa Qala, we had a six-hour stopover at FOB Edinburgh where I joined the other lads in 3 Troop, who all made me feel very welcome. In fact, they made me feel as though I had always been part of the team. I slept in the Mastiff that night, and the following morning, after Frankie and Scotty showed me the ropes of my new job, I was involved with the rest of the Troop in providing force protection for the Brimstone (Royal Engineers mine and IED clearance) and our own Op BARMA teams, who cleared a route green (safe path) to Musa Qala for the convoy.

As I was soon to discover, clearing a route green is a long job, with our lads in four-man Op BARMA teams on foot with Vallon metal detectors sweeping the path in front of the vehicles, marking the safe passage with spray paint and identifying the site of possible IEDs for the ATOs (Ammunition Technical Officer of the bomb disposal team) to clear.

As the column made its way slowly from FOB Edinburgh to Musa Qala, I drove the Mastiff up to an OP, on a hill overlooking both the wadi and the route to our destination. We watched the whole convoy pass, before rejoining on at the back. The journey was less than ten miles, but it took all day, and we didn't reach the tank park in Musa Qala until late afternoon. There we unloaded and made the vehicles ready for the next day. I met up with our Troop Leader, Lieutenant Barney Campbell, and eventually Frankie and Scotty showed me to the Squadron's accommodation tents, where I bunked next to Jerry's driver, Kenny Bell.

As I soon found out, Musa Qala was not only home to the Household Cavalry Regiment's 'C' Squadron, Regimental Headquarters (RHQ) and some of 'A' Squadron in Jackals (a four-wheeled, open-topped armoured vehicle, armed with a 0.50-inch Browning Machine Gun). It also held a unit of the Royal Artillery equipped with a 105 mm L118 Light Gun, a towed howitzer, known to us and the Taliban as a 'Dragon gun'. Unlike Camp Bastion, everything was very basic, although there was a gym, a helicopter landing pad, a big mess tent and all the back-up services that go with armoured vehicles in the field.

The garrison in Musa Qala was on the Forward Line of Enemy Troops (FLET), tasked with pushing the Taliban out of Helmand and Afghanistan. Within that task, 'C' Squadron was deployed with its Mastiffs to provide force protection for the lads on the ground. 3 Troop, when we were later equipped with our Scimitars, would be additionally tasked with providing armoured recce and flank protection. Musa Qala itself was surrounded by a ring of Patrol Bases (PBs), manned by men from the Royal Anglian Regiment (known as the Vikings) and the Yorkshire Regiment (known as the Yorks), with some of our units in support.

And what were my first impressions of Afghanistan? Well, it certainly wasn't Barbados, which is lush, green, rolling, and surrounded by sea. In stark contrast, Afghanistan is arid, yellow, mountainous, and landlocked. We may not have great roads in Saint John, but as I'd just experienced on the drive to Musa Qala, tarmac is also in short supply in Helmand. And it was very, very dangerous everywhere. I've read that warfare is characterised by long periods of boredom, interspersed with brief periods of high anxiety. That may be true of a conventional war, but in my experience, it falls well-short of describing an insurgency, where you are continuously surrounded by an enemy who are indistinguishable from the locals, and whose principal weapon is a concealed IED. From the day I arrived in Musa Qala until late-November, I was mostly engaged in the clearance of these deadly weapons, rather than in direct fighting with the Taliban, although there was some of that too.

My first encounter with an IED was an interesting one, made more so because I wanted to actually see and experience an explosion. We were providing force protection for a Brimstone IED-clearance team, tasked with clearing a village. They had found a device on the opposite side of a building to where I was parked up. Over the radio, I heard that the ATO was going to conduct a controlled explosion. This meant that everyone in the area had to take cover or get inside their vehicles; but I was having none of that and wanted to see what was going on. In spite of being told in no uncertain terms to get down inside the Mastiff, I stuck my head out of the turret. It was a relatively small IED, but even with a building between us, the pressure wave generated by the controlled explosion was immense. The blast gave me a nose bleed and one of the worst headaches I have ever had. None-theless, I still had to drive the vehicle back to Musa Qala. It served me right.

That was not the end of the excitement. On the way back, and full in my line of sight, Jerry McGuire's Mastiff ran over an IED in a wadi. The blast was horrific. Worse still, I knew that the Commanding Officer, Lieutenant Colonel Harry Fullerton, and the Regimental Corporal Major (RCM) Adrian Gardner, were travelling in the back. They were the two top men in the Household Cavalry Regiment. It would be a miracle if they were not injured, but fortunately they were unhurt. When the smoke cleared, I saw Jerry standing on the roof of the Mastiff, with his arms outstretched and the biggest smile imaginable on his face. It was his way of putting two fingers up to the Taliban; but his vehicle was so badly damaged that, when it was safe to do so, the Colonel and the RCM had to transfer to my Mastiff for the rest of the journey. Instead of the hour it had taken us to drive out, the return leg took five hours as our Op BARMA teams found more IEDs between my Mastiff and Jerry's wagon. That day was definitely my moment of reality in Helmand.

Not long after this incident, we heard that 3 Troop's CVR(T)s were at last ready for collection, so we were flown in a Chinook from Musa Qala back to Camp Bastion to collect the new wagons. We spent three days there, taking over the vehicles and preparing them for service, which included zeroing the 30 mm RARDEN cannons. This also gave me the opportunity to catch up on some sleep, see a few friends, and reconnect with lots of good food.

The convoy back to Musa Qala was uneventful, as far as action by the Taliban was concerned. This was perhaps because as before we were shadowed all the way by Apache helicopters. However, it was not without its problems for me. Sitting in the driver's seat in the Scimitar, with the hatch open, I ate dust. Combined with the terrain, that brought on the motion sickness I had first experienced in the earlier Mastiff driver training. I repeatedly had to stop to be sick, and it was only by gulping down pints of water and juice that I managed to make it to FOB Edinburgh. There I stuck my head into one of 'C' Squadron's tents and created a near riot. It was only when I was handed a mirror, I realised that my face was completely yellow with dust, except for two black patches around my eyes. I took a much-needed shower. Then somewhat surreally, given where we were, I watched Arsenal playing Aston Villa: my team, Arsenal, won. The rest of the journey to Musa Qala was as uneventful as before. It's difficult for me to over-emphasise how good I felt about being back with the Squadron in the driver's seat of a new Scimitar. After all, this was what I had joined the Army to do. Mastiffs were all very well, and I was recognised as a good driver, but they were troop carriers, not fighting vehicles. I took an immense pride in that Scimitar, which ran like a dream.

While in Afghanistan I always carried a Bible with me. With Mr Campbell's support I tried, not always successfully, to get the other lads to say a short prayer with me before we went beyond the wire. So far, the power of prayer had kept me safe. Just before our next patrol, we heard intelligence reports of a potentially large number of IEDs on our route, and I prayed that extra bit harder.

The intelligence report proved to be correct. Later that day while returning to base, I suddenly heard a sort of 'boof' sound. Frankie told me to get my head down inside the Scimitar, so he could traverse the turret over my head, and Jerry who was in the wagon behind us yelled 'STOP!' My vehicle had run over an IED, but had only triggered the detonator and not the main charge. One of the rear idler wheels carrying the track was damaged, but the wagon was driveable. However, worse was to come.

Two or three hundred meters to my front, I saw Mr Campbell's Scimitar coming back towards us. Without warning there was a massive explosion next to his wagon. Mercifully, he and the rest of his crew were unhurt, but the CVR(T) was badly damaged. Not for nothing was the Squadron's radio call sign 'Titanium'. We quickly realised that we were in the middle of an unmarked field of IEDs. It was *not* a good feeling. Mr Campbell immediately radioed base for a Quick Reaction Force in Mastiffs to help us out, and, eventually they were able to clear a route back to Musa Qala.

After that incident I was given my yearly appraisal by Mr Campbell. He said he was very pleased with the job that I was doing in the Troop, asked me what I would like to do in the future, and told me that I was 'off the board' (which meant in line for promotion). Meanwhile, my mind was firmly fixed on my upcoming two-weeks of R&R in the UK. Once again I flew in a Chinook to Camp Bastion, and then boarded C-130 bound for Kandahar, where we switched onto a civvy flight that took us back to England. My departure had been over-shadowed by the news that Richard

Ward in 'A' Squadron had lost both his legs in an IED explosion. We had joined HCR at the same time, after serving together at Knightsbridge.

...

Just before Christmas, I was due to return to Helmand for the second part of the tour. This time I found it even more difficult to tear myself away from Marketha, the girls, Sissy and my mum, both of whom had flown over from Barbados to be with my family over the holiday. Never before had I missed a family Christmas. To make it even more difficult, I had instantly fallen in love with our new baby, Alexa, and didn't want to leave her; and the money problems had not gone away either. I had already decided to deal with *that* issue when I got back to Camp Bastion, by signing on for another four years and collecting the bounty. However, in the meantime, the taxi was waiting outside. I stood in the girls' bedroom and looked at them sleeping. 'We are going to be OK,' I said to myself, then turned and left the room. Marketha stood on the pavement and watched me, as the taxi set off for the barracks.

Once back at Camp Bastion, I signed my service extension papers. I also heard that Ben Hilton of the Coldstream Guards had lost both his legs above the knee while I was away. I had known Ben at the Mounted Regiment, where he worked in the Household Division Stables, and he was my neighbour on the patch in Windsor. This awful news, so close to home, bothered me a lot.

After flying back to Musa Qala in a Merlin transport helicopter, I quickly got back into the 'C' Squadron routine, patrolling between OPs and providing force protection for IED clearance. On Christmas Day, however, operations were put to one side and we enjoyed a proper Christmas lunch with turkey, mince pies, and all the trimmings. It was spoilt only by a rumour that in the near future there was to be a big push to clear the Taliban from the area to our south. Like all good Army rumours it turned out to be true, as the first phase of this operation was indeed in the region south of Musa Qala.

Although still officially Frankie's Scimitar driver, for this one operation I was assigned to drive the regimental doctor, Surgeon Lieutenant Colonel Jedge Lewin, in a Mastiff. This wagon was fully equipped as an ambulance and was on the command radio net, so I could hear everything that was going on. First, with much regret, I had to temporarily hand over my new Scimitar to Trooper 'Dangerous' Dave Porter.

As soon as we had deployed, there was a massive IED strike on a Mastiff, three or four wagons in front of us. It was commanded by another of my neighbours on the patch, Staff Corporal 'Nudger' Newell. The wagon was a write-off, no one was hurt, but it had to be recovered. While this was going on, the convoy halted, and I heard over the net that Andy Phelan was a casualty. He had been hit in the stomach and back by flying debris when a chopper landed on the Helicopter Landing Site (HLS) he was controlling. Andy was seriously injured and had to be casevac'd (Army slang for casualty evacuation); I was completely gutted by this news. Once the convoy got going again, we moved to an overnight leaguer (laager?). There we waited until all the troops were in position for a very big daybreak attack to clear the Taliban out of a nearby village.

The following morning, with mild weather and clear visibility, I drove the ambulance to the top of a hill overlooking the operation. Once there, we could not only hear on the radio net the action as it unfolded but, from my position in the driver's seat with Colonel Lewin next to me, I could actually see it happening through the armoured glass windscreen. This was my first such experience, and it made for crazy watching and listening. I could see Taliban dickers (target spotters) on motorbikes on high ground, giving instructions on short-wave radios to their fighters in the village. This 'icom chatter' (Taliban radio traffic) was being monitored by our terps (interpreters), who were simultaneously briefing the operation's commander via the net on the Taliban's intentions.

I could also see our infantry clearing through the village, supported by 3 Troop's Scimitars. Then helicopter gunships roared in, as the dickers directed Rocket-Propelled Grenades (RPGs) at Corporal of Horse Craig

Harrison's Troop, mounted in Jackals. He was the first casualty to be brought to us, having been hit on the helmet as his Troop was smashed up. Craig was a sniper, who earlier in the day had recorded the longest-ever kill (to that date), by taking out two Taliban machine-gunners at a range of 2,707 yards, which is over a mile-and-a-half. It earned him the nickname of 'Long Shot', and later he published a book about it titled *The Longest Kill*.

Then I heard over the net that 3 Troop was advancing through an irrigated field. 'Don't let him throw a track,' I said to myself, which is precisely what 'Dangerous' Dave then did by trying to make too sharp a turn in wet ground. 'That's my wagon!', I yelled, 'what a dickhead!' Worse was to come, for the REME LAD, led by Corporal 'Ads' Stores, had great difficulty recovering my Scimitar. Worse still, the recovery slowed up the whole action.

We drove back to Musa Qala with no further casualties, and there was a lot of humorous banter on the net, which is not unusual in such circumstances. However, I was not in a funny mood. Far from it: I was fuming at the damage that had been done to my Scimitar. Once we parked up, I asked Colonel Lewin if I could go and check-out my wagon. The closer I got to it, the angrier I became; I had handed over a Scimitar in perfect running order and now it was damaged. The red mist descended and I was ready to lose my shit with 'Dangerous' Dave, but before I could do so, Jerry McGuire, who never wanted conflict in his Troop, intervened.

However, if the vehicle was to be ready for operations the next day, it needed a lot of work doing on it. So, I metaphorically rolled up my sleeves and Scotty Porter, our gunner, said that he would help. We worked on the wagon for hours, cannibalising a redundant Sultan (CVR(T) command vehicle) for spare parts, until we had fixed it. That, however, was not the end of my problems on that day. As Scotty and I were working on the Scimitar, I suddenly felt a searing pain over one eye. I looked up and saw an Afghan kid holding a rock. A product of his environment, he laughed and ran off. Even if I had wanted to respond, we were ordered to ignore such actions by the locals. In some ways, the locals of Helmand unwittingly helped us because they always made themselves scarce when Taliban action was about to 'kick-off'. We would then see the dickers deploying on their motorbikes, although we were not allowed to take them out until they opened fire on us.

Within a couple of days, the rumours started up again. This time the talk was that we were to be deployed to the north, around Patrol Base (PB) Woqab, which was held by the Vikings, and that we would be accompanied by Afghan Police who were being trained by the British. Woqab lay in the shadow of Mount Musa Qala, a huge red mountain quickly re-named Mount Doom by the lads because it was straight out of *Lord of the Rings*. It was a really kinetic area (meaning a high activity military action zone). The talk – and there was lots of it – was that the upcoming task was going to be even bigger than our previous action to the south.

In the event, our Troop was part of the operation to push the Taliban beyond Woqab. This task included establishing a new Patrol Base (to be known as Habib, after an Afghan soldier who had been killed there) on the top of a hill called Horseshoe Ridge to the north of and overlooking Woqab. This feature had never been seized before and was an entrenched Taliban stronghold, from which they could observe our every movement in Woqab. But before we could clear the Taliban off Horseshoe Ridge, we had to get there.

The nearer we got to our objective, the more kinetic it became. However, because of all the shit that was flying around, we were stuck in a queue waiting for the ground which we wanted to take to be cleared. Once it had been, and we were at the top of the hill, I closed my hatch as a serious fire fight had started. I wasn't on the regimental radio net, so I couldn't hear what was happening, but I could certainly hear strikes on our vehicle. I asked Frankie if stones were being thrown at us. 'No,' he said, 'that's small arms fire.' Then he told me the terps had established from the icom chatter that there were dickers on Mount Doom, who were directing fire onto us.

It was then that the firefight got really hot. Our Scimitars were pouring 30 mm fire onto an identified Taliban compound across a wadi from us, in which there were a load of fighters, while the Gunners (Royal Artillery) starting firing their 105mm Dragon gun. Jerry, who on this particular day was commanding a Mastiff, was in support of the Vikings and hit an IED. He was unhurt, but his wagon had to be recovered later. During a lull in the fire fight, Colonel Harry joined us, and almost immediately we were engaged once again by the Taliban. Shortly afterwards, our attack was given close air support by an A10 Warthog jet, armed with its awesome 30 mm Gatling-style gun, and an Apache helicopter, which fired its Hellfire missiles. By the time they left the scene, the Taliban compound was completely destroyed. Things then settled down, which allowed the Sappers (Royal Engineers) to start building PB Habib's defences using massive Hesco barriers.

While we were in the Patrol Base, we slept out under the stars in bivvy bags (waterproof sleeping bags). As in Canada, these seemed bigger and brighter than when we were in camp. It was actually rather magical. One night, I climbed onto one of the Sapper's tractors to get a good signal, and called Marketha on the satellite phone. I could hear very real distress in her voice. Although she was paying the bills, the financial situation back home was not good; the bounty still hadn't come through, and she was being hassled by the bank. There was nothing I could do about it.

In the following days, we erected a tent at PB Habib and life settled down into a routine, but not for long. One day, I was standing on the top of my wagon when I heard explosions in the distance and saw shit being kicked up, which was gradually getting closer to our position. Far from bricking myself, I continued to stand there watching it, swinging my helmet in one hand. 'What the fuck do you think you are doing, Mapp?' Mr Campbell roared at me. 'Get your helmet on and get under the wagon! NOW!' I dived under the Scimitar and shouted back to him to tell Scotty and Frankie that I was there, so they wouldn't drive off and crush me to death.

At that moment, earth and rocks started flying in all directions as enemy mortars landed around the waggon. Thank God, none struck our vehicles but Lee Brooker, a REME craftsman in our vehicle recovery Section (part of the LAD), got hit by shrapnel in his legs as he tried to climb into the Samson (the CVR(T) recovery vehicle, known as a 'Sammy'). I got peppered by flying debris, but with no real damage done. Lee had to be flown out later and it was only then we discovered that the Sammy was parked over an unexploded IED. During that time, we also had intermittent incoming rifle fire on our position. On one stag (sentry duty), I at last got to fire the RARDEN cannon at the enemy, using the infrared night sight. When not on duty in the Scimitars' turrets, we huddled behind the Hesco barricades where we brewed-up (made tea), cooked and chatted.

In the meantime, information came in on the radio of events beyond our PB, including the awful news that one of our ATOs, Captain Dan Read of the Royal Logistic Corps, had lost both legs and an arm while clearing a booby-trapped IED behind Habib. Captain Read was an incredibly brave man, who had already been injured by an IED earlier in the tour, and had at great danger to himself cleared the IEDs off Horseshow Ridge. The medics on the ground managed to tourniquet Captain Read's wounds and move him to Woqab, where he was to be evacuated to Camp Bastion. Sadly, despite everyone's best efforts, he died before a helicopter-borne Medical Emergency Response Team (MERT) could reach him. It was a very solemn day that followed. To say that we were all upset would be a considerable understatement.

However, before we knew what had happened to Captain Read, my wagon was ordered to the HLS to provide protection for the casevac. The site was surrounded by trees, and as it came in to land, one of the Chinook's rotors hit a branch and the chopper was grounded. Later, Captain Read's body was flown out on an Angel Flight by a smaller helicopter. Meanwhile, I stayed with the broken Chinook, until it was repaired and flown back to Camp Bastion. I drove back to PB Habib in a very gloomy mood.

One of the remarkable things about Helmand was that, just before we cleared a village of Taliban, it would become as silent as the grave; but afterwards it would return to normality quite quickly. If I needed a justification for being there, that was it. However, as life got back to normal in the liberated villages, we knew that the surrounding villages and roads were still, quite literally, a minefield of unmarked IEDs. Private Mark Allen of the Vikings, and several others, had their legs blown off in a series of incidents. Our attitude to the Taliban was not improved when they nailed these and other severed limbs to trees.

I may have been carefree earlier on this operation, but by now I knew that my Scimitar would soon have to move forward. Faced with the prospect of driving over ground that was riddled with IEDs, I reassured myself that Frankie, Scotty and I would be behind a Mastiff. When a Major from the Vikings told them that he would be calling for our support the following day, I knew that meant we would be moving into shit. I spoke to Marketha on the satellite phone that evening and told her I was worried about what might happen next. She tried to talk to me about her problems, but I wasn't listening. Later, that really bothered me.

As predicted, the following morning some of 3 Troop, including my Scimitar, were ordered to support the Vikings, who were clearing a village in front of us. Unlike previous days, I didn't say my morning prayers or talk to God, and I was definitely not myself on the morning of 31st January 2010. Anyway, I drove the Scimitar into the convoy formation behind Jerry's Mastiff, with Scotty on foot in front of us, checking the route for IEDs as part of our Op BARMA team. He was armed with a Vallon metal detector and a large aerosol can of yellow paint, with which to mark the cleared passage. We knew that there were IEDs ahead, because we had seen the locals moving in a certain, familiar pattern, which led to some pretty dark-humoured banter on the radio. I freely admit that I was worried, because I thought we might get smashed; but I was resigned to whatever might happen.

We had moved some way down the road. Although we weren't yet under fire, I asked Frankie in the turret if he wanted me to close down, so he could traverse the gun, but he said not to. Then we heard that a sergeant from the Viking Company, who was mentoring the Afghan Police, had been shot in the head, was pinned down by dicker fire, and couldn't be moved. My Scimitar was ordered up on to high ground, so that we could provide protection for an improvised HLS for the casevac. As we moved, we too came under fire. Once again, I asked Frankie if I should close down so he could swing the turret. 'No, no, don't bother,' he said, 'I'm turret surfing'. Sitting on top of the turret was a safer place to be than inside the vehicle, when the threat of IEDs was greater than small arms fire. I remember thinking that we were in a bad place when . . .

CHAPTER 8

Operation MINIMISE

FROM THAT MOMENT and for the next three weeks, during most of which I was in a coma, I can recall absolutely nothing. So the story of what happened after the explosion, and until I came-to in a bed in Selly Oak Hospital, has to be told first by Jerry McGuire, who saw it happen, and then by my wife, Marketha, who had to deal with the consequences.

Staff Corporal Matthew 'Jerry' McGuire's story
During that tour in Afghanistan, I was Corie's Troop Corporal of Horse; and on 31st January 2010, I was also his Troop Leader, as Mr Campbell had returned to the UK for a course. Corie's Scimitar, with Frankie Francis in the commander's seat and Scotty Porter in the gunner's, was that morning behind my Mastiff, as we moved along a track in support of the Vikings, who were tasked with pushing back the Taliban's FLET.

From our FOB, we could see that the ground to our immediate front was clear, but there was a dead spot beyond that, caused by a turn in the track which also narrowed at that point. Because of this, it was necessary for me to order Corie's Scimitar ahead of my Mastiff, and so I told my Op BARMA team to dismount and start clearing the ground. This was already underway, when I received a call to give fire support from some high ground to our front right, for the casevac previously described by Corie. I told the boys to take it carefully. As Frankie edged past me, with Scotty in front of the wagon with a Vallon, I gave him the 'thumbs up'. Frankie was one of those absolutely fearless lads, who had been utterly reliable during the whole of the tour to date. I want to put it on the record that I was fortunate to have him and Blakey as vehicle commanders. They were both good friends. Along with Mr Campbell, who was a great Troop Leader and really valued his men, the leadership of the Troop was as good as it gets.

The Scimitar hadn't gone more than twenty or thirty yards, when I heard rather than saw a huge explosion. From that moment, everything seemed to go into slow motion. At first, all I could see was a big cloud of smoke. As this cleared, I saw a bivvy that had been rolled up on the left side of the Scimitar floating in the air. Beneath it was what remained of the wagon: the turret had been blown off, as had the tracks, the running gear, and most of the armour plates on the driver's side.

Without thinking of the danger from other IEDs, I jumped down from the Mastiff and started to run towards the wreckage of Titanium-Three-Three (the call sign of Corie's vehicle). At that moment, the Vikings' 'A' Company Sergeant Major (CSM), Iain Collins, appeared on a quad bike, dismounted and, joined me as I ran. The first crewman I saw was Frankie, who had been blown at least twenty feet clear of his turret, and was lying on the ground. Of mixed race, and never short of words, Frankie was as white as a sheet and completely silent, but obviously in great pain. I checked him over and although he seemed to be intact, I knew that he might have internal injuries. In fact, it later emerged that he had a broken pelvis. 'Stay there and don't move,' I ordered him; then I ran on. The next man I saw was Robbie 'Geach' Mcgeachy, one of our Op BARMA team, who told me that Scotty was on the track ahead: 'He's screaming and in a lot of pain, and he's also covered in yellow paint.' 'What about Corie?' I asked. 'He's fucked,' came the reply.

As Geach went off to tend to Scotty, I found Corie lying on his back on the ground by the side of the wrecked Scimitar's hull. He'd been blown out of his seat by the force of the IED. If he had been closed down, he would have been killed instantly. His helmet was still on and he appeared to be grinning, which was odd as he was completely silent. Then I saw that what I'd thought was a characteristically cheeky Corie grin was his teeth showing through a gash that ran right across his face. It was only then that I realised he'd lost his left leg below the knee and the other one was really badly smashed up and hanging by a thread. You may think it strange, but my first thought was that this was not as bad as it might be. We frequently joked that it was better to lose a leg below than above the knee, as far as rehabilitation was concerned. As another of the Op BARMA team applied tourniquets to Corie's legs, I checked over the rest of his body, and saw that his jaw and left hand were also not in good shape. He was awake, but not really conscious. Realising that he would soon be in great pain, if he wasn't already, we gave him a shot of morphine, which we all carried. I marked his forehead with an 'M' and wrote on it the time it had been administered. Then I went to check out Scotty. When I reached him, he was covered in yellow paint and looked just like Homer Simpson. This was an image that he later took a long time to live down. Although he was hurting badly, he didn't appear to have any major external injuries, which was later confirmed. Nonetheless, it was clear that he needed immediate hospital treatment.

While Lance Corporal of Horse Sam 'Blakey' Blake from another of the Mastiffs stayed with Frankie, and the Op BARMA team cleared a safe path to him, Iain Collins had gone back to collect his quad bike. This was equipped with two stretchers, onto which Corie and Scotty were gently loaded. As this was going on, I went back to my Mastiff to transmit a MIST report. This gave the Ops Room the Mechanism of injury, i.e. IED; Type of injury; Signs (pulse etc); and Treatment (morphine, tourniquet etc). They in turn sent a 9-liner report to Camp Bastion. Then, as Iain drove the quad bike back to the FOB, I followed in the Mastiff. By the time we got there, a team of guys was waiting to move Corie and Scotty to the HLS at PB Habib and I went with them. We arrived at Habib just as a Chinook was landing. As Camp Bastion was forty minutes flying-time away, it must have been somewhere in our area, which was really fortunate. No sooner had it touched down, than the rear ramp was lowered and I helped carry Corie's stretcher on board. As I laid it on the floor of the Chinook, Corie looked up and although he doesn't remember this, through the gash in his face he spoke:

'Have I lost my legs?' he asked. 'You have,' I replied, 'but below the knee, so you're going to be OK.' He then tried to hug me.

As soon as Corie and Scotty were safely stowed on board and I was back on the ground, the rear ramp was raised, and the Chinook flew off to Camp Bastion. I returned to the site of the IED to deal with the aftermath. We were a very close-knit Troop and this incident hit all of us badly, but we held together.

The next day we returned to Musa Qala and I had the job of packing up Corie's kit. For some reason, I didn't want any help with this task, which tells you a lot about the way I felt about Corie and what had happened to him. That same evening, I called my dad, who lived in Birmingham. I told him what had happened, and asked him to look in on Corie, Frankie and Scotty, and send me progress reports, which he did on several occasions. This enabled me to give updates to the Troop on our injured friends' conditions, and much faster than would have been possible through the official channels. Everyone was very grateful to my dad for doing that.

It's a grim fact that I was blown up three times on that tour, and that doesn't really bother me. But I'm not ashamed to admit that I still choke up when I remember that day.

Marketha Mapp's story

When Corie returned to Afghanistan just before Christmas, I moved our three girls into our bedroom at 3 Lyell Walk in Windsor, so that we could keep each other company at night. On that Sunday morning of 31st January 2010, I got up, still in my pyjamas, and went down to the kitchen to make a pot of tea for all of us. I think the kettle had just boiled, when there was a ring on the front doorbell. I went to open it and there were two men in suits. I didn't know either of them, but I could see that one was a minister; the other I later found out was the Casualty Notifying Officer. My stomach hit the floor, for whoever they were, they could be there for only one reason: 'Don't let him be dead,' I prayed. 'Don't worry, he's not dead,' one of them said, without me even asking, 'but he has been badly injured. May we come in?'

I showed them into the sitting room, but before they could tell me what had happened to Corie, the shock brought on my asthma and I started hyper-ventilating. One of them, I don't remember which, ran off to find my inhaler. Once I'd had a few puffs, I was better able to deal with the news that they had to give me. This was that Corie had been very badly hurt, and that his injuries included losing his left leg at the scene of the IED explosion. Immediately afterwards he had been flown to Camp Bastion, where his right leg had also been removed. They went on to tell me that he would arrive back in the UK the following day, Monday 1st February 2010, and would be taken straight to the military wing of the hospital at Selly Oak in Birmingham. Corie was stable, but very ill and in a coma.

I don't now remember the exact order in which things then happened, and I certainly can't recall when I changed out of my pyjamas. But once I had taken all this in, we started to discuss the arrangements for the next days and weeks, during which I was assured that all the costs would be taken care of. The officers told me that I would be driven by a regimental Casualty Visiting Officer (CVO) to Birmingham the next day, to be with Corie. But what about the girls, I asked? Lexi (Alexa) was just a baby, but the two older girls, Erin and Jodie, were in school. Clearly, I needed some help.

It was then that the regimental welfare and support system really came into its own. With the officers' help, and with the support of my friend Cammelia, who rushed down from London to be with me, we worked out how we were going to manage while Corie was in hospital. I agreed with the officers that I had to contact our family in Barbados, not only to tell them what had happened, but also to see if some of them could come to Windsor to help out with the girls.

To cover the time that I would be spending with Corie before the family arrived, it was quickly arranged that my neighbour at 1 Lyell Walk would look after Lexi, and my neighbours on either side of me, at Nos 2 and 4, agreed to be temporary child-minders for Jodie and Erin, dropping them off and picking them up from school. I was then told that as soon as our family had arrived from Barbados and settled in, I would stop the daily commute to Birmingham and move to a hotel near the hospital, until Corie was discharged. And that's exactly what happened.

At some point on that awful morning, I told the girls the awful news. This was tough, as Jodie and Erin were old enough to understand and could anyway see that I was very upset. My initial thought was to withhold the whole truth from them, but then I decided that they had a right to know, and that with my support, they would be able to deal with it. So holding back the tears that otherwise flowed all that terrible day, I explained to them as gently as I could that their daddy had been badly injured. I then told them that he had lost his legs, but he would be coming home and he was going to be alright – although at that time, there was no certainty of that outcome.

Probably after I'd told the girls, I called our family in Barbados. I didn't want to give the news over the telephone to Corie's mum or his sister Sissy, who was like a second mother to him, as I was really worried about their reactions. So, instead, I called Sissy's husband, Wayne, and asked him to tell them face-to-face. This he did and it was quickly arranged that as soon as they could, Sissy, Corie's mum (Pinky), Jackie, and my mum (Ucelia), would fly over to be with us.

Before any of that happened, on Monday 1st February I was taken by the CVO to see Corie. When I walked into the Intensive Care Unit, I didn't recognise him, until I saw the bull's head tattoo on his arm, that he'd had put on as a tribute to Dwayne Johnson. He was not a pretty sight. Covered in bandages, his left hand was suspended above the bed, he was hooked up to drips and drains, and I could see immediately that he had lost both legs. I was then told that, as well as the amputations, his jaw had been broken; his lower lip had been severed in the blast, but had been stitched back on; he had a punctured lung, and his left hand was badly damaged, with the knuckles broken and protruding.

I stayed with him for a few hours before being taken back to Windsor. This was a routine that was repeated daily until our family arrived, after which my mum stayed in Lyell Walk with the two older girls, and I moved to Birmingham with Lexi, Sissy, Jackie and Corie's mum, Pinky. At week-ends, we all got together to be with Corie.

Each day that Corie was in the coma, we would sit by his bed, holding his hand, stroking his head, talking to him and telling him stories. In fact, we stayed with him until he was discharged from the hospital and sent to Headley Court for rehabilitation. However, and this is the most remarkable thing, although he was very ill and could well have died from trauma or blood poisoning, from the moment that he came out of the coma he started to make a very rapid recovery. So fast was his return to life, that within a week of regaining consciousness, the drains were removed from his stumps, he was put in a wheelchair, and he spent the evening with us in the hotel. Shortly after that, he was discharged. From the time of the explosion to that discharge, Corie had been in hospital for just one month: it was a miracle.

And that's really all there is to tell. But before handing the story back to Corie, I think it's worth saying that, although it may have been more than ten years ago and my memories of the events of that first day are a bit of a blur, my memory of my emotions is not. Whenever I think about it, it's as though I have just opened the front door of 3 Lyell Walk on Sunday 31st January 2010.

. . .

While Jerry's recollections of 31st January are all in slow motion, and Marketha's memories of what happened after that are a mix of emotions, my own memory of those days after I came out of the coma are multi-layered: clear, but at the same time a bit jumbled up. Everything seemed to be moving in parallel rather than in sequence. Part of the reason for this must have been the drugs I was on, particularly morphine with which – as I found out later – I was being accidentally over-dosed and to which (although nobody knew it at the time) I was allergic. But that cannot have been the only reason. However, this book is not a stream of consciousness narrative, but a record of what happened, how and when it happened, and how I felt about it at the time. This has forced me to get my memories into some sort of order.

On waking-up two weeks after the explosion, and after the initial confusion, it didn't take me long to get my bearings. The ICU bay I was in had one other bed in it, occupied by Captain Martin Driver of the Vikings, who had been with us at PB Habib. Although he was very badly smashed up, I recognised him immediately. Sadly, he later died; but that was after I had been moved two days later onto Ward S4, the other inmates of which were mostly from the Household Cavalry Regiment. Captain Andrew Jelinek was there with a broken back, as was Richard Ward, the double amputee from 'A' Squadron, and Clifford 'Cliff' O'Farrell who had broken legs. Clifford had been 'Long Shot' Harrison's spotter when the sniper had acquired his nickname. One of the few non-Household Cavalrymen was Corporal Ricky Furguson MC of The Rifles, who had lost both legs, several fingers, his left eye, and some of his mouth. I was also told that Frankie and Scotty were in the hospital, but on a different ward.

Despite the horrific injuries of the men on S4, or perhaps because of them, the banter was pretty extreme, particularly when we were told that we had to smarten up for David Cameron, who was electioneering and doubtless wanted a good photo for the next day's papers. When I was told that I had to shave, I gave a one-word answer: 'Ridiculous'. On another occasion, I think it was my second day on S4, one of the Military Liaison staff in the hospital, who was himself a single above-the-knee amputee, also told me that I needed to shave. If I could have done, I would have booted him in the face.

Most of the nurses were angels, but there was one whom none of us liked and we set out to make her life a misery. We deliberately waited until she had settled at her desk, and then we would take it in turns to demand her attention. It was good for our morale, but must have been hell for her, as we intended. That's wounded soldiers for you. There were also some hilarious moments. Richard Ward's wounds were being cleaned by leeches and one night they escaped. The next morning some of us, including me, looked as though we'd just come out of a mangrove swamp.

Those are the good memories of my time on S4. However, beneath the stiff upper lip that I showed to the lads, inside I was both a physical and a mental mess. Physically, I felt like shit and had no appetite. In fact, I only managed to eat the odd slice of pizza in those first few days. There was also something wrong with my blood, and although I appeared to be healing well, the doctors wanted to get to the bottom of the problem. To do that, they had to take me off all my medication, including the very strong pain killers that I was being given. The hours that followed were hell. Then one night, I woke and needed to go to the toilet. Forgetting that I had no legs, I tried to climb out of bed, fell and split open a wound on my right stump. That too was bloody painful.

On I think the third night, I told my sister Jackie, who was sitting with me, that I was feeling super-bad. She was already really worried about me. This was because I had told her the day before that my past life had replayed itself in my head, and she had interpreted this as a prelude to my death. 'I feel sick,' I said, and then, without warning, projectile-vomited the entire contents of my stomach over her and a nurse who was nearby. The mess was awful and included not only half-digested pizza, but black bile, which was probably blood, and – unbelievably – sand. It was a turning point, for after that it seemed that all the bad stuff had left my body. I started to eat anything and everything I could lay my hands on, and I started to feel *physically* better.

Meanwhile, on the mental side matters were bad. I kept telling myself that my career was over, and that I couldn't be a father to my girls, who any- way would probably be horrified at my injuries. When I had told Jackie about my life passing before me, I had also said: 'What's going to happen to me?' As Geach had told Jerry: I was fucked. I felt no better after I was visited by the man from Pax Military Insurance, who told me that my financial worries were over. 'So what?' I thought, if I didn't have a life. Marketha got me to start looking online for properties in Barbados, where I planned to move the family. But to do what? If that was bad, there was worse.

I vividly remember being wheeled into a shower the day after I was put on S4. It was my first proper wash (other than bed baths, I suppose) since the explosion three weeks before. I should have enjoyed it, but I was in bits. As the water rained down on me, the tray filled with my diluted blood, and when I started to shampoo my hair, it came out in clumps. That was the last straw and I started sobbing. I don't know how long I sat there, but at last the nurse who was waiting outside knocked on the door. 'Are you alright?' she asked. I wouldn't reply. She asked again and I yelled back: 'NO!'. With that the door flew open and she wheeled me out. 'Let's get you back to the ward,' she said, as she dried my back. 'Why did this have to happen to *me*?' I asked in despair. Before she could reply, I dumped all my misery onto her.

Later that day, I wasn't feeling much better, when Kath the Cake Lady (Kath Ryan), who still runs Cakes 4 Casualties, came onto the ward with her trolly. She was really lovely and made me feel a bit better. Then a physiotherapist came to see me and asked if I wanted to work out. 'No, go away,' I told her. In fact, lots of people came to see me in those first two or three days, all determined to buck me up, but I wasn't to be taken out of my misery. The first were Frankie on crutches and Scotty, now scrubbed clean of yellow paint. They had seen me in a wheelchair, just as I was arriving at S4; it was weird seeing them – a sort of good weird – and we hugged, but I couldn't cheer up. Jerry's father, John McGuire, came in every day I was in hospital, for which I am eternally grateful.

Another of those early visitors was Mr Campbell: 'I'm really sorry that I wasn't there for you,' he said. I could see he was really devastated that, not only had he not been with his Troop, but all the burden of command had fallen on Jerry at the very worst moment. The pain was written all over his face. I told him, and I meant it, that it was a privilege to have been one of his Troop. Then he made me laugh, really laugh, and that helped, but it still wasn't the end of my depression. An unexpected person who tried to buck me up was the regimental Second-in-Command's mother, Mrs Philipson-Stowe, who visited me several times. She was great. Best of all, however, were Cliff O'Farrell in his wheelchair and Captain Jelinek. Knowing that I was in the same boat as them helped, but I was still not out of the woods.

Then I was told that Captain Sean McMullen, the regimental Welfare Officer, was bringing my girls up from Windsor to see me. Before they arrived, I shaved and showered, and tried to make myself look my best. As

I was wheeled into the families' sitting room, where they were waiting for me, instead of the look of horror that I had dreaded, their faces lit up with joy. 'Daddy,' shrieked Jodie, 'I know you are injured, but you'll get some metal legs and teach me how to ride a bike.' It wasn't a question; it was a life-affirming statement. It was also my mental turning point. If my girls thought that I was still the same man as before, why should anything be any different? I can't now remember what else was said, but I do remember that we spent the rest of that wonderful evening laughing and joking. Later, one of the nurses said: 'We can see that you are feeling a lot better.' I was. 'Can I see the physio tomorrow?' I asked.

When she rocked up the next morning, I was full of energy and my body was telling me 'Let's get going again, buddy.' 'I'm ready,' I told the physio, 'Let's go and work.'

At around this time I was visited by Lieutenant Colonel Rhodri Phillip, who was to be my consultant at the Defence Medical Rehabilitation Centre (DMRC) at Headley Court. He told me what to expect there. He was accompanied by a prosthetics guy called Ian, who measured me for the cups on my new legs and gave me some Juzo compression socks to wear on my stumps.

The Saturday that followed I spent with the family at their hotel, and then on the Sunday 28th February 2010, Captain McMullen took us all to Headley Court, which I was to attend, on and off, for the next two years. My face had healed, I needed no more reconstructive surgery, I was free of stiches, and I had identified a plot of land to buy in Barbados. You see, the moment that I had settled my physical and mental problems, I had started to mend in mind and body – and to do so at a speed that amazed the doctors. Marketha has said that it was a miracle. Who am I to dispute that? Actually, I sincerely believe that in the darkest of those days, God took over the running of my body when I was incapable of doing so. Now, I was ready to get back on my feet.

Back on Two Feet

THE DEFENCE MEDICAL Rehabilitation Centre (DMRC) at Headley Court, near Epsom, was established at the end of the Second World War for injured Royal Air Force pilots. In 1985 it became a tri-service facility. Today, it no longer exists as, in 2018, it was moved to a much larger set-up near Loughborough, becoming the new Defence and National Rehabilitation Centre at Stanford Hall in Nottinghamshire.

When I arrived at Headley Court in 2010, it was staffed with specialist medical officers, nurses, remedial instructors, physiotherapists, occupational therapists, speech and language therapists, a cognitive therapist and social workers. The rehabilitation areas included hydrotherapy pools, gymnasiums, and workshops for prosthetics. Unlike a hospital, the patients there were weekly-boarders, going home every week-end to be with their families, and the treatment and training operated on a two-weeks-on/ two-weeks-off cycle. As I was to discover over the next twenty months, it was a very remarkable place.

On arrival, and after filling out loads of paperwork and being subjected to several examinations, I said goodbye to my family and tried settling into the four-bed bay on which I had been placed. Having also left my mates behind in Selly Oak, I felt very alone and rather low. The staff tried to cheer me up, but it was only once I had discovered how to access the Sky Sports channel that I started to feel better.

I had already set myself four goals for those early days in Headley Court. As soon as possible, I wanted to be able to drive a car with a manual gearbox; I was determined to drive to-and-from my house in Windsor on a daily basis, rather than be a boarder; I intended to be standing at Combermere Barracks for the arrival back from Afghanistan of my Squadron, scheduled for later in March; and I promised myself that I would be on parade, in uniform, on the Medals Parade to receive my Operational Service Medal for Afghanistan. These were not modest targets, as I was then still in a wheelchair.

On Monday 1st March, my first day at Headley Court, I faced a session with a psychiatrist. It did not go well. I really resented the way that he talked to me, and the way that he seemed to be playing games with my mind. If this was psychoanalysis, I was having none of it, and because I was really angry, I told him so in terms that I can't repeat here. So much for psychiatrists. My next session was in the gym, where I was scheduled to have my first fitness session and meet my Exercise Rehabilitation Instructor (ERI), Kelly Thistlethwaite. That went much better, particularly as it included introductions to some of the other lads in rehab. Things were definitely looking up, and they improved still further when I met with my occupational therapist, an ace guy called George Glew, who sorted out my first wheelchair.

Then Ian, whom I'd met at Selly Oak, presented me with a new set of legs. In no time at all, I had them fitted and stood up. It was agony. 'Don't worry, the pain will pass,' Ian said. 'More importantly, before you can race around on those legs, you need to understand and then re-learn what you have lost which, for a start, is your balance.' Finally, I met my physiotherapist, Kate the Aussie (as she was known). She was a wonderful person: soft-spoken and kind, but someone who immediately understood how to push me. Very early on, I told this team of the goals that I had set myself. 'I'm not going to make any promises,' Kate said. 'Just don't tell me, 'no',' I replied – and she didn't.

Instead, those four brilliant people supported my hopes and dreams, and by the end of that first week I was walking short distances unaided. It's the simple truth that Kelly, George, Ian and Kate (until she returned home and was replaced by Helen) were the team who got me back on my feet. I owe them.

After that first day, I quickly got into the routine at Headley Court, which operated like a school, with a fixed timetable for all the activities. The day started at 8 a.m. with breakfast, followed by circuit training in the gym, sessions with George and treatment from Kate. It was all really enjoyable and made more so because of all the banter with the other lads. In the round, the purpose of this programme was to teach each of us how to function once again as a normal human being. The fitness classes gave us strength and stamina, and the occupational therapy sessions refreshed our old skills and gave us new ones. While I was at Headley Court, I took part in cooking and hypnotherapy, learnt to play golf and the skills of sitting volleyball, and I got back to grips with cricket.

In addition to the physical and new skills stuff, we went on regular outings into the surrounding towns, where we shopped in supermarkets (not easy in a wheelchair), visited gyms to assess which equipment we would be able to use (once we were back full-time in the community), and started planning the changes that would need to be made at home to accommodate our disabilities. These sound like very simple things to do, but they weren't - at least not at first - which was I suppose the point of doing them in the first place.

As my mobility improved, Kate and Kelly became like my sisters. I trusted them totally, even when things went wrong. Kate worked with me to achieve functionality with my new legs, including how to walk, climb stairs safely (the trickiest skill to learn), walk on different surfaces, and eventually how to run. She also told me when to stop, if I was about to overdo the work at the *barre*, and she worked on the soft tissues in my stumps, which led to one really painful moment. While massaging one of them, she hit a nerve ending. We were both caught off guard and I flew off the massage table screaming. Even though I felt as though a red-hot poker had jabbed into me, reducing me to rubble and Kate to tears, the other lads in the treatment room thought it was hilarious and ribbed me unmercifully.

That's Headley Court for you – and none the worse for it – and the end result of this abuse was howls of laughter from all of us, Kate included. A couple of months later, when Kate the Aussie returned home, she was replaced by Helen. She was also an absolute sweetheart, but she pushed me even harder. This included getting me to walk up and down Box Hill on my new legs. *That* was a challenge.

Kelly the ERI focussed on getting me fit, with independent sessions lifting weights and doing cardio-vascular exercises She also taught me how to ride a bike using my new legs. In those sessions with her I learned yoga, swimming, and lots of other skills to help me back onto my feet. Fortunately, she was my instructor throughout the twenty months that I spent in rehab at Headley Court.

One of the first occupational skills training sessions for me was driving, which was provided by a lovely little old lady who would turn up at Headley Court in a Ford Fiesta. Once I was behind the wheel wearing my prosthetic legs, she would check that I could use the clutch, the brake, and the accelerator pedals safely. She also needed to know that I could make emergency stops, although we never actually did one in a safe area. This was because at a roundabout in Epsom, on the way to an off-road space, some dickhead cut me up, and I had to do an involutory emergency stop. 'Well,' said my instructor, as she rocked back in her seat, 'you seem to have mastered *that* skill already.' By the end of the week, her hair was whiter, but she was satisfied that I was as competent behind the wheel as I had ever been, so that was one of my initial goals achieved.

Did all this training and therapy work in time for the return of 'C' Squadron from Afghanistan? The short answer is 'yes'. On the day that my mates were due to arrive in buses at Combermere, I was collected from home by Captain McMullen and left outside the NCOs Mess. As I had promised myself, I was *standing* there in civvies as the transport pulled up, the guys dismounted, grabbed their bags, and piled into the Mess. It was a great moment. Afterwards, we had a beer-fuelled reunion which included Franky and Scotty. I couldn't have been happier.

And what about the Medals Parade? That too I also achieved in the way that I had planned. For this event, all my family were there, along with my best friend, Renier Grace. He and I used to speak on the satellite phone when I was in Afghanistan, and he'd been quite amused by the sound of gunfire he could occasionally hear in the background: 'Is that close to you, dude?' he had asked. 'No,' I lied, 'miles away.' He was determined to be present on this day and had flown over specially. As I got into uniform for the ceremony, he helped me to put on my boots.

My progress to stand and walk on my new legs was very quick. This was not because I was a super-fast learner, but because I thought that the associated pain was to be expected, and so I didn't report it. Had I done so, my instructors, therapists and trainers would have slowed me down, and I might not have achieved my goals of standing to welcome back 'C' Squadron and being on parade to receive my campaign medal. There is a lesson there somewhere, even if it is a painful one.

Looking back at it, my time at Headley Court can really be divided into two halves, separated by Christmas 2010 when I took the family back to Barbados. Before that holiday I was fully engaged in the rehabilitation programme, reconnecting with the Regiment, and sleeping at Headley Court on the weekdays while I was there. After I got back, I commuted daily, thereby achieving the last of my initial goals, and I was largely engaged in competitive sport.

Very early on I had asked George, 'What's next for me?' He had replied 'Anything you want.' Well, there were lots of things that I wanted, but it seemed to make sense to start with those things that I was good at *before* I lost my legs. Cricket and volleyball were my two most obvious sporting skills, so I focussed on those, while adding golf to my sports bag. Sport at Headley Court was used to rebuild self-confidence, but it was also a rehabilitation tool, particularly for hand-eye coordination and balance.

I also had to address both my home life and my career. Neither was straightforward. As our new house in Barbados began to rise from the ground, we had to think about where we wanted to raise our kids. Clearly,

I could take British citizenship and stay in the UK; or with my new-found financial independence, go back to Barbados and rebuild a life there. The UK was the home of my dreams, but Barbados is my real home. However, the fact that I wanted to stay in the Household Cavalry, and they seemed to want to keep me, tipped the scales – at least at first.

At no point had I been taken off the strength of the Regiment. It seemed to me that all I had to do was report for duty and make myself available for work, whenever I was not required to be at Headley Court. But what was I to do? My first preference was to re-join 'C' Squadron, go on a Skill-at-Arms course, and then become part of the Training Wing at Combermere. This was not thought to be a good idea, as the hierarchy worried that young soldiers being taught by a battle casualty might have a negative effect. I suppose they had a point.

With that path blocked, I asked if I could return to duty at Knightsbridge. To underline the request, I applied to go on a riding course at the Royal Military Academy Sandhurst, which was specifically designed to get injured servicemen with riding skills back in the saddle. By the end of a week's training, I was doing all the things I had done while serving at the Mounted Regiment, including controlling a horse at every pace and jumping. I could see no reason why I shouldn't go back to ceremonial soldiering and take my place on Escorts and Queen's. The Riding Master thought otherwise, saying that it was one thing to control a horse in ordinary riding kit, but it was quite another when encumbered with a helmet, cuirasses, sword, and jackboots. Again, I suppose he had a point. The sight of a Household Cavalryman being binned on parade is not a good one, whether or not he has prosthetic legs. It could be life threatening, as the then Colonel of The Life Guards, Field Marshal Lord Guthrie, found out when he was rushed to hospital having fallen off his charger while returning from The Queen's Birthday Parade in 2018.

So, what was I to do? Eventually it was suggested that I learn a new skill, that of tailoring. I didn't object, and was put onto the QM's strength and started working in the Tailor's Shop. If you want to know how I *actually* felt about this, you can do no better than to watch the 1956 film *Reach for the Sky*, starring Kenneth More as Douglas Bader, a young RAF officer who had lost both legs in a flying accident. In a sequence following his rehabilitation, and in spite of having passed a flying test, Bader is told he cannot return to the air as there was 'nothing in the book' about legless pilots. He was also told he could stay in the RAF, but he would be grounded and deskbound. Bader left the RAF, only to return at the start of the Second World War and go on to be a fighter ace. I decided to stay in the Household Cavalry.

In July 2010, something happened that encouraged me to take this decision. I was stitching away in the Tailor's Shop, when the Orderly Corporal appeared and told me that I was on that day's Colonel's Orders, which was about to start in Regimental Headquarters (RHQ). 'Shit,' I thought, 'what the hell have I done?' Colonel's Orders is the daily disciplinary parade at which fines and penalties are handed down for minor misdemeanours, or referred to higher authority if they were more serious crimes. When I arrived at RHQ there was a queue of lads lining the stairs, but I was ordered to the front. 'Can you drill?' demanded the Regimental Corporal Major when I got to the top. I said that I could. 'Right,' he said, throwing the Colonel's door open, 'Trooper Mapp ... Quick March ... Halt ... Salute ... Trooper Mapp, Colonel.' Standing behind the desk, which I'd almost fallen over when I halted, was Lieutenant Colonel Harry Fullerton. 'This is a very proud moment for me,' he said, 'congratulations on your promotion, Corporal Mapp. You *really* deserve this', he added, as he handed me the badge of rank of a Household Cavalry Lance Corporal.

I slipped the sleeve, on which were two stripes and a crown, onto the flap on the front of my combat dress, saluted and marched out. I felt about ten feet tall. Back outside the Colonel's office, the RCM was waiting for me. 'We're really proud of you,' he said, putting his arm around my shoulders, while all the lads started clapping. I had managed to hold back my emotions in the Colonel's office, but that clapping was almost too much for my self-control; nonetheless, I just held it together. It had all been a complete surprise, and I was blown away as no IED could ever have done. If I thought that was the end of it, I was mistaken. As I entered the QM's department, all his staff were waiting for me and there was more clapping, cheering, and hugging. Then I was handed my instructions for joining the NCOs Mess, including a reality check: the details as to how I was to pay my future mess bills.

The next big event was an extended Christmas holiday in Barbados. For this I set myself a new goal of going home on my own two feet, without taking a wheelchair, crutches or a walking stick with me. And that's exactly what I did. But this was not to be a simple holiday visiting family and friends, inspecting the building of the new house, and lapping up the sun. In addition to all of those things, I had to deal with the sheer emotion of going back, and then get through a programme of public events. These started with the annual Barbados Independence Day Parade, to which I went as the guest of Lieutenant Commander Clarke of the Barbados Defence Force. It was the first time I had worn No 2 Dress with my new rank and campaign medal. After the parade, I was taken back to the Officers Mess, where I was introduced to the Prime Minister and senior officers, some of whom I had served with in the Cadets and the Reserves.

This parade was followed by visits and talks to the Royal Barbados Police Force and the Barbados Defence Force. At a meeting with the Commissioner of the Royal Barbados Police and his senior staff, he told me that if I needed anything they would have my back. One of the talks that I gave was to my old unit in the Reserves. It was well received, but afterwards in the Q&A session, there was a bit of push-back from some of the lads, who questioned why I had gone out to Afghanistan in the first place. 'The job of a soldier is not to question his orders,' I replied, 'but to get on and do the task he has been set, to the best of his ability. That's what I did – and I'm really proud of it.'

Luckily, I did not have to make these visits and give all of these talks on my own. This was because I had arranged that Mr Campbell (who by now was a Captain, but I always think of him as 'Mr'), Regimental Quarter Master Corporal Warren Brown (my boss in HQ Squadron), Corporal of Horse Paul 'Doc' Holliday (the Master Tailor), and Jerry McGuire, joined me a week later. They were given the services of a police car and driver, and were housed as guests of the Barbados Coast Guard. Together, we attended a reception at Garrison Secondary, during which Mr Campbell and I both gave short talks, and then handed out replica Afghanistan campaign medals, some pace sticks, and a few pairs of drill boots to members of the Cadets. I used this and other talks to encourage the kids to think outside the box, and to aim high, by telling them about my dreams and how I was fulfilling them. However, it was not all visits and talks. We were invited to a reception at the High Commission, hosted in our honour by the British High Commissioner, Mr Paul Brummell; we were given evening cruises around the island on the MV *Harbour Master*; and I took my colleagues to see the sights of Barbados, including Harrison's Cave, which is a spectacular underground grotto in the middle of the island with a subterranean lake, and loads of stalactites and stalagmites.

After Mr Campbell and the lads from HCR left for the UK, I took Marketha to Sandals in St Lucia for a week's rather delayed honeymoon; it was definitely worth the eight-year wait. She and the girls then flew back to the UK. I had one further task to perform before I also returned to Windsor. That task, one of the most significant of my life, was to stand as Renier's best man at his wedding, as he had done for me when I married Marketha. I can't describe exactly how I felt: all I can say is that it was an absolutely awesome moment. In a neat piece of unintentional symmetry, the opening moments were a repeat of my own wedding, except that this time it was Renier who was sobbing with nerves outside the church, and it was me who had to pull him back together.

On my return to Windsor, I soon discovered that things were not likely to pan out with the Regiment as I would have liked. This got me to thinking about possibly returning to Barbados, and we decided that Marketha would go back there with the girls in July 2011, initially without me. This was not only to organise our new house and to put the girls into school in Barbados, but to give them a chance to learn about their heritage and culture. Meanwhile, I remained in the UK to finish my rehab and to focus on elite sport and the time I had left in the Regiment.

During my rehabilitation, my early engagement in team sports, principally cricket and sitting volleyball, was largely down to one man, who became very important to me. Sergeant Alex Menya of the Adjutant General's Corps was on the staff at Headley Court. Born in Uganda, he was the manager of the Battle Back sitting volleyball team, for which he was later awarded an MBE. I first met Alex when he was on the coaching team for Army Volleyball. Although not his job, out of the kindness of his heart he looked out for me while I was in rehab. When I was really low, it was his shoulder that I cried on. By way of thanks, I once took him for a drive to Epsom in a red-and-white Ford Mustang that I had acquired as part of my own, private recovery programme. It may have been the speed at which I drove, or the interior's psychedelic light show that was a feature of this car, but it was an experience he didn't ask me to repeat.

It was Alex who encouraged me to take up disabled cricket and sitting volleyball. Both of these were adaptive sports which I was skilled in before I went to Afghanistan, particularly volleyball which I had played for the Army. However, although some of those old skills were useful, I had to learn a whole new set in order to compete. Fortunately, these came to me quite easily, and before long I was playing cricket for Hampshire County's D-40 disability team.

On the sitting volleyball front, my big break came when I met Ashley Trodden at Stoke Mandeville's 2011 LimbPower Games. Ashley was the assistant men's coach for Team GB. He watched me play, believed in my potential, and invited me to join the training camp at Bath University, where British Paralympic athletes were preparing for the London Paralympic Games of 2012. This was so that I could experience an elite sport environment. I didn't compete in London 2012, but in 2013 I was in the sitting volleyball teams for Team GB, the British Armed Forces team and the Battle Back team. Colonel Tristan Crewe, one of the physios at Headley Court, introduced me to golf, and once I'd mastered the balance problems, I thoroughly enjoyed it. I even joined the Battle Back golf team, and played in the USA on courses in Florida and San Antonio, Texas.

Towards the end of 2011, Colonel Phillip got me to focus on the end game. This, he said, was the moment I would leave Headley Court and get on with the rest of my life without their support. I had a meeting with him every Friday while in rehab, during which he reviewed all aspects of my progress towards independence. At this particular meeting, he said: 'You are not going to be here forever. It's time to crack on and secure your independence.'

But for me there was a problem: although I wanted to stay in the Army, I didn't want to be a military tailor. All of which begs the questions about when I found the time for my military duties. The answer is that, with the Regiment's encouragement, I had become what is known as a 'tracksuit soldier', a description which speaks for itself. The Army has always been willing to make time for soldiers to play sport, and to turn a blind eye when competitive sport at an elite level meant the soldier spending long periods away from barracks. The reasons are easy to see: serving soldiers winning sporting medals is good for morale, profile, and recruiting.

The Household Cavalry's treatment of para-athlete sportsmen in its ranks was no different to that of its approach to the able-bodied. Budding champions were to be encouraged, and I was given extended leave to train for the 2012 Paralympics. However, that year I decided I needed to step back from elite sport and focus on creating my new life by spending more time at home and playing golf locally, rather than being abroad or at training camps for long periods. That said, I did attend the London Para-lympics as a potential athlete. This, and my later visit to the 2014 Winter Olympics at Sochi, was part of the Paralympic Inspiration Programme, known as PiP, run by H4H and the British Paralympic Association.

It is worth noting at this point, that I also received support from the Household Cavalry Foundation (HCF), a charitable trust established by serving and former members of both The Life Guards and The Blues and

Royals, to look after their soldiers, veterans, their dependants and the Regiments' retired horses. In the days following my injury, it was the HCF that paid to bring my family from Barbados and to keep my family by my bedside. Once I was in rehab, and up to the present day, the HCF has also supported my sporting activities, alongside Help for Heroes (H4H), Blesma, and Rupert Fryer, who I will come to later. I have nothing but praise for the HCF. Along with my former comrades-in-arms, Jerry McGuire and Mr Campbell, they have always looked out for me and continue to provide support. They are all brilliant.

I can't fault the Household Cavalry's welfare regime, and the Regiment couldn't have been more supportive of my elite sporting commitments. Nor do I regret one second spent serving The Queen. However, the manner of my leaving the Regiment was abrupt to say the least. I have since learned that they had no choice but to medically discharge me, but I'm still sore that I was told of the decision without any warning. I'm not going to go into the details, as this book is about aspirations, but on hearing the news, I marched out of the new Commanding Officer's office and went straight home, never to return to Combermere Barracks in uniform. Before drawing a curtain over that one negative incident, I will say this. Brutal it may have been, but with hindsight I needed that moment to make me focus on what I was going to do next. But what was that going to be and where?

CHAPTER 10

Playing to Win

ONCE THE ARMY decided that my future no longer lay with the Household Cavalry, there seemed little point in continuing to live in Windsor. Anyway, the presence there of so many soldiers would constantly and painfully remind me of what I had just lost. Marketha had stopped working when I was injured, and she had returned from Barbados with the girls in February 2012. As she was still not working, there was no need for us to live in any particular place. Although a move from Windsor would mean the girls changing schools yet again, that seemed like a price we would have to pay. However, wherever we were to settle had to be a long-term move, as the girls in particular had suffered enough disruption and needed to put down some permanent roots. Of course, there was the option of returning to Barbados which I will always regard as my real home, and where we had the new house. But it had become clear to me on my last visit that the island simply didn't have the medical facilities I might need. The prosthetics unit at the Queen Elizabeth Hospital in Bridgetown was little better than a poorly equipped tool shed, and there were none of the disposable peripherals that I needed, such as gel pads. I tried to help with this situation by asking the team at Headley Court to send their used prosthetics to Barbados, but that was not a solution for my needs.

Although it was a hard decision for us to make, Marketha and I agreed that we would use Airbnb to rent out our new house in Barbados to provide us with some extra income, and we would then search for a house to buy in England. Our criteria were quite straightforward: any property had to be easily adaptable to my needs, be located in a thriving community, and have good road and rail connections to London. The Army agreed to extend our tenure in Windsor while we looked, and our search took us to view properties in the London suburbs, in Kent, and even in Windsor. Nothing was suitable. Then we found on-line a newly-built house for sale in a development in north Swindon. It was within our budget, there were schools for the girls within easy walking distance, excellent local shopping, and good connections in all directions. On my iPad it looked ideal, but would the house meet our needs?

As I walked in through the front door, I knew immediately that it was perfect. A helpful, ex-military sales agent made the process of buying easy, the girls were registered with the local schools, Marketha quickly got a good job with the local NHS, and I found a local gym and a great fitness coach, Anna Greco, with whom I've been working ever since. Until the time, at some point in the distant future, when we decide to spend more time in Barbados, the house in Swindon is our home and has become more so since my sister Jackie and her family moved from Barbados and bought a place down the road from us.

We moved into our new home in Swindon in October 2013, and put our own mark on the place in a way that we had never been able to do in a service quarter. We were helped enormously by the arrival of Jackie's son Jesse, who was studying at Oxford Academy. I drove him to school on Mondays and collected him on Fridays, and at the week-ends, he took on the heavy-lifting, helping me to put up shelves, hang pictures, and do the hundred-and-one other things necessary to turn a house into a home. When not doing those jobs, he helped Marketha with the girls. We could not have done without him.

So, with life on the home front settled – at least for the time being – what was I to do with the rest of my life? The answer that immediately presented itself was competitive sport, and I threw myself into it to the exclusion of almost everything else. With the benefit of hindsight, I realise now that I was trying to prove to myself that the loss of my legs was no obstacle to making my life a success. My intense focus on this later had consequences. However, I should now state something that colours everything I do in sport: I *always* play to win, and – as will become apparent – I have a real problem with people who think it's OK to lose.

As for the sports I engaged in, although I have played in golf competitions here and in the USA, it has always been for me a leisure activity. I plan to continue to improve my handicap, but I will never play at an elite level. Disabled cricket was a different matter, particularly as while I was in rehab I'd properly fallen back in love with the game. Battle Back cricket at Headley Court took me to Uganda, on a tour organised by Alex Menya, where we played against their national team. In our downtime, we visited an HIV hostel for kids, which was an experience I won't forget in a hurry. It wasn't long before I was selected to play for the Hampshire County Cricket D-40 team, which took me to pitches around the UK and to two National Championships. However, my involvement with competition cricket came to an end with the last game of the 2014 Championship. We were in the closing overs of the game, and all we had to do to win was to 'bat time' and stay focussed, as I told the next man in. He ignored my advice, played wildly, and was immediately clean bowled. 'I let you down,' he said, as he passed me on his way back to the pavilion where Mike Gatting was watching the play. 'I don't want to hear this,' I thought. The next man in was called Jack. He had a hand disability, but he did as I advised, played cautiously, and we won. As we celebrated, Captain TA's C Drills kept running though my head, and I reflected that the team was too easily distracted by our opponents. That was the last game of competitive D-40 cricket that I have played. I still love the game, but . . . Besides which, in 2014 sitting volleyball and bobsleigh were consuming increasing amounts of my time. Which brings me to my involvement with sitting volleyball, the Paralympic sport that I'd been encouraged to play by Alex Menya while in rehab. Unlike a lot of other disabled players, I had the advantage of having played volleyball competitively, and at a reasonably high level, as an able-bodied athlete. All that I had to learn (and it was a lot) was how to play the game while sitting on my bottom, and without the aid of legs. In 2013 I played in several competitions. The first was the National Cup played on Paralympic Day at the Olympic Village in the East End of London. I was playing for Team GB. Although we lost miserably to the Netherlands (and deserved to), it was a really proud day for me. For the first time, my family had seen me play for my country, and I could see on the faces of my kids what it meant to them. Next on my sports agenda was the Warrior Games in Colorado Springs, USA, where I played for the British Armed Forces Sitting Volleyball Team.

While I was there the wheels of my new way of life started to wobble. I had only been at the Games for two days, when I got the news that Marketha was unwell. I flew back to the UK immediately. This is probably the right moment to explain that, unintentionally, my focus on sport to the exclusion of everything else was having repercussions at home, particularly on Marketha. I was physically and emotionally changed from the man she had married; my old dreams lay in ruins; and I needed to find myself. To do that, I needed some space. Like many severely injured servicemen, I also felt the need to be with people who were in a similar situation to myself; and I was focussing solely on competitive sport as a route back to normality. All of this took me away from home for long periods of time, with the result that Marketha felt increasingly isolated, which was not good.

Back in the world of elite sport, the next item on my 2013 agenda was the European Championships in Poland in which I was part of Team GB or, to give it its correct title, the Great Britain Sitting Volleyball Team. With unresolved issues at home, I was not in a good place at the start of this competition and, to be absolutely blunt, I hated the tournament. There I was in Poland, yet again away from home for an extended period, and for most of the Championship I was kept on the side line. Worse still, I couldn't understand why I wasn't being allowed to play, until I realised that our coach had lost faith in my abilities. When that penny dropped, the wheels came off my self-confidence and esteem, which was much more fragile than I had ever let on.

It all came to a head before the closing ceremony, ahead of which I'd

been drowning my sorrows in beer and vodka. By the time we were supposed to march on, I was so pissed that I was, quite literally, legless. The
following morning the team manager gave me a monumental bollocking
that was wholly deserved: it was one thing for me to feel unjustifiably
treated and appallingly sorry for myself, but it was quite another thing to
let down my country in such a public way. I apologised unreservedly. In the
weeks that followed, the old coach was replaced by a new one, Branislav
Kovac, with whom I built a good relationship and who helped to rebuild
my confidence in my ability to play. But I never again competed for the
national team in a major competition.

Nevertheless, I was still very much engaged in the sport with the Battle
Back sitting volleyball team, formed at Headley Court and sponsored by
H4H. Initially created as a sport recovery tool, it had at some point become
serious from a competitive point of view, and got more so as time went by. In
fact, there were two Battle Back teams: the A Team, which competed in
national championships; and a B Team for beginners. Needless to say, I was
on the A Team, and travelled with it to San Antonio in Texas, throughout
Europe, and to various training camps and competitions around the UK.

In 2012, I had in fact been appointed the captain and manager of the A
Team. In that role, I was determined that the rest of the players should be
as serious about winning as I was. I now recognise that this was a mistake.
Not everyone involved in Battle Back sitting volleyball was as single-
minded as I was, and that created very real tensions. The situation was
eased when Charlie Walker was appointed our coach in 2013. An ex-Team
GB player, who later coached the British Armed Forces Sitting Volleyball
Team at three Invictus Games, Charlie was a great guy. Although we
would often bang heads, his training helped us to win the 2013 National
League. Not long after, and because of my other commitments, I was
replaced as captain and in 2014 I resigned as manager. My time with Battle
Back sitting volleyball was at an end and I wasn't sorry, but it was not the
end of my involvement with the sport.

At the 2014 Warrior Games in Colorado Springs, and before I had to fly home, the British Armed Forces Sitting Volleyball Team won a Bronze medal by beating the US Navy team. I was also on the Track-and-Field Team at that Games for the 100 meter, 200 meter, and the 4 × 100 meter relay sprints. I only managed a fourth place in the first two, but the 100 meter relay went into the history books. Ours was an all-amputee team and thereby hangs a tale. First off the blocks was Kushal Limbu, a double below-the-knee amputee Gurkha, who ran his heart out and handed the baton to Dave Henson of the Royal Engineers, a double above-the-knee amputee and Paralympic Bronze medallist, who in turn handed it to me. I think I ran reasonably well, and we were certainly in with a chance of a medal, when I handed the baton over to Matt Webb of the Royal Marines. Matt is a triple-amputee, having lost an arm and both his legs above the knee. As I approached Matt for the handover, I completely forgot that with no knees of his own, he would be much slower off the mark that I was. As I got closer to him, he didn't seem to be moving, so I shouted 'Move – MOVE!' Shortly after, with Matt still slow to get going and me unable to stop on my blades, I ended up tackling him rugby-style. As quickly as I could, I helped him up and then ran his lap with him. We were last – but we got the biggest cheer.

My appalling cock-up in the sprint relay at the Warrior Games, was followed by an altogether more successful participation in the Invictus Games in September of that year, which I will describe in a moment. However, before I do so, I want to digress onto a related subject about which I feel very strongly.

It is a fact that charities, and Help for Heroes in particular, have given enormous support to wounded and disabled servicemen. Without their help and money, I would not have been able to achieve much that I have done and I am eternally grateful to all of them, particularly the Household Cavalry Foundation. However, it is also a fact that in some (but not all) of these charities' politics, with a small 'p', has become an important feature. That is a game that I have never been willing to play and it has caused me not only problems but also great hurt. I'm not going to name names, but on more than one occasion, I have been aware that things were being said behind my back that no one had the guts to say to my face. I am not imagining this. One particular day, I was waiting to speak to someone at one of the more prominent of these charities, when I overheard the following conversation: 'I must go, I have to see Corie Mapp.' 'Poor you, I hear he's a right arsehole.' He may have been right, but the person who said this was able-bodied. He had never had to undergo the physical and mental trauma of people like me, whose lives – through no fault of our own – have been blown apart in the service of our country. The job of these charities is to help to put us back together again, not to be judgmental about the people we had involuntarily become. The men and women who join these organisations need to understand the challenges they will be facing, particularly having to deal with badly-damaged individuals with severe mental and physical problems. If they regard working with us as just a job, or a stepping-stone to something better, then they are in the wrong place.

Which brings me back to the Invictus Games, which is the polar opposite of what I have just recounted. Most people know that they are the brain child of Prince Harry, who had officially opened the 2013 Warrior Games. He then decided to develop and widen the concept into an international competition for disabled servicemen around the world. It is not widely known that he established the Games in the teeth of strong opposition from the powers that be, and that his vision for the Games was much greater than just the establishment of an international competition. The proof of this lies in the application process. Unlike for the Paralympics, or any other competition for that matter, to compete in the Invictus Games everyone is required to complete a written submission, the contents of which are every bit as important as the person's sporting prowess. In particular, potential participants have to explain not only *why* they should be in the team, but also *how* it would benefit them as a person. This makes the Invictus Games different – and quite extraordinary.

To date, I have participated in three Games, the first of which was held in London in 2014, using the facilities built for the 2012 Olympics. The experience of being immersed into a diverse group of serving and ex-service men and women, drawn from every campaign since the Falklands War of 1982, was both uplifting and humbling. I am fortunate that my injuries are purely physical, but while in the Olympic Village for that Invictus Games, I met and exchanged experiences with people who have PTSD, other mental illnesses, and physical injuries that could not be corrected with prosthetics. Although our experiences and disabilities were widely different, the emotional and physical pain that we have endured was the same. The truly remarkable thing about the Invictus Games is that, by creating a forum for the exchange of views and experiences, it really helps individuals to cope better. That is the healing power of the Invictus Games.

Equally important is the way in which when a competitor is struggling – because of a personal injury, an accident, or simply an equipment failure – the other competitors instinctively rally round to help. The military commitment to never leave a man behind is very much a part of the Games. That, too, makes it different to almost any other competition that I know, other than the Warrior Games, although I readily acknowledge and salute the triathlete, Alistair Brownlee MBE, who gave up his chance of winning the World Triathlon Series in Mexico in 2016, in order to help his brother Jonny over the line to a second-place finish, coming in third himself. Alistair Brownlee's selfless action was unusual in an able-bodied competition, but is absolutely the norm at the Invictus and the Warrior Games.

At a personal level, the Games taught me that you don't have to have a label to be a leader. I was captain of the sitting volleyball team for the 2014 Games, but not in the two subsequent ones. At first that hurt; but when there was an issue with which I could help, I unhesitatingly stepped up to the mark, as did others. And why not? The point of participating in a competition, whatever your level, is to do your best for your Regiment, your country and your family. You can't do that if you think only of yourself.

On a more general level, I believe that the Games give us wounded veterans the opportunity to show those who helped us, in the immediate aftermath of our injuries, that their help was not in vain, and that it produced positive, life-enhancing results. When I won a Gold medal for sitting volleyball, one of the first people to congratulate me was Lieutenant Colonel Rhodri Phillip from Headley Court. It was he who started me on the path leading to that medal, and he deserved it as much as I did. I hope, in that moment, he recognised that fact. If he didn't, then he will now. In summary, the Invictus Games is unlike anything else, given the benefits it brings to wounded servicemen around the globe. If Prince Harry does nothing else with his life, then the establishment of the Games is a testament to his compassion. It is also a monument greater and more worthwhile than anything achieved by most men, and something of which he can and should be mightily proud.

My own involvement in that first Invictus Games was diverse. I applied to compete in sitting volleyball, track-and-field, and wheelchair rugby. In the event, I competed in the first two categories. In the 100 meters sprint, the only track-and-field event in which I actually participated, I came second from last. Getting a good start off the blocks using blades is difficult, and some of the other runners were on their own legs. But I'm not making excuses; the best man won.

For me the main event was the sitting volleyball, particularly as I was the team captain. We trained hard, with weekend camps at Bath University, the National Volleyball Centre at Kettering, and Tedworth House in Wiltshire, which is part of the Defence Recovery Capability partnership between H4H, the Royal British Legion (RBL) and the UK Ministry of Defence. We also played matches in the National League at which we honed our competitive skills and acquired the edge we would need. By the time the Invictus Games opened, we were capable of performing at the highest level. I felt utterly exhilarated by the experience of leading the British Armed Services Sitting Volleyball team into the arena for the first game.

For the duration of that competition, we were accommodated in an amazing five-star hotel. More amazing still were the support staff and the public, who between them created an atmosphere that I can only describe as fantastic. That, and our training, carried us through to the final for the Gold Medal, which was against the US team. As that game progressed, and we started ramping up our score, I could see that the Yanks were becoming increasingly demoralised, and this was cumulatively impacting their game. I wanted us to win on merit, not because of a dispirited opposition, particularly as they were a really good team that had temporarily lost its way. So, I tried to encourage them. 'This isn't you,' I called across the net, 'pick up your heads and fight!' And they did, although I'm happy to say we won. On the podium or just afterwards, Prince Harry came over, gave me a hug, and said: 'It's wonderful to see you smile.' 'It wouldn't have happened without you, mate,' I thought, but didn't say. Once a Life Guard always a Life Guard, at least when it comes to respect for the Royal Family.

In the two Invictus Games that followed, we won Silver medals: the first in 2016 in Orlando, Florida, against the US team, which was back on form; and the second in 2017 in Toronto, against a team from Georgia. However, the 2014 Invictus Games was my last sitting volleyball competition as captain. I continued to compete, but my focus switched away from sitting volleyball because of pressures at home and the issues I had with the national game. By the autumn of 2014, I had cut my ties with disabled county cricket and reduced my commitment to sitting volleyball, in favour of my new obsession with bobsleigh – the purest form of insanity.

CHAPTER II

The Purest Form of Insanity

COMPARED TO GOLF, volleyball, sprinting, cricket and rugby, the sport of bobsleigh is less widely understood, so a word or two of explanation is called for. In much the same way that, in 1823, William Webb Ellis picked up a football during a game of school soccer and ran with it, thereby creating the game of rugby, the sport of bobsleigh was invented sixty years later by Englishmen on a winter holiday at Caspar Badrutt's hotel in St Moritz, Switzerland. Quite who had the bright idea of fixing two of the local delivery boys' sleds together with a board, in such a way that the front sled was steerable, is not known. It is recorded, however, that the new sleds were used by Mr Badrutt's guests for competitions down the icy streets of the town, until the locals started complaining. In order to keep both his guests and the townsfolk happy, Badrutt had an ice-run built on a steep slope outside the town, near a village called Cresta, and the sport of bobsleigh was born.

Although popular from the start, formal competitions only began on the Cresta Run in 1884. The International Bobsleigh and Skeleton Federation (IBSF) was founded in 1923, but the sport was part of the first ever Winter Olympics the following year. Modern tracks are standardised at 1,200 to 1,300 meters in length, with at least fifteen corners, one straight and one labyrinth (three corners in quick succession without a straight section). As speeds can exceed 75 mph, the gravitational pull on some corners is as much as 5-G, and there have been seventeen fatalities in competition since 1907. Bobsleigh is not for the faint-hearted.

Para Bobsleigh took longer to develop, and it wasn't until 2010 that the

IBSF formed its Para Sport Committee, and the first international competition was held in 2013 in Latvia. The current international competitive calendar now includes the World Championship, run as an annual four-heat race held on a single track, and the World Cup, awarded on a cumulative point score achieved at ten, two-heat races held on different tracks (although in the early years there were fewer venues and races). At the time of writing, a decision on whether or not Para Bobsleigh is to be included in the 2026 Winter Paralympics is still pending. Various disabilities qualify a person to pilot a mono (one-person) sled in these competitions. However, to ensure a level playing-field, and unlike in track-and-field, leg amputees are *not* allowed to wear prosthetics.

I knew none of this when the sport was first suggested to me at Headley Court in 2012; indeed, some of it had not even materialised then. But I did know that bobsleigh involved hurtling down an open-topped ice tunnel. 'No way,' I said, 'I'm broken enough already.' Nonetheless, the rehab guys persisted saying that I should try it, because I had good hand-eye co-ordination. Eventually, I agreed. In late-2013 I set off for an international training camp in Calgary, a place I knew from my time in Canada with the Household Cavalry Regiment. With me was Matt Richardson, a Gunner whose feet had been shattered by an IED in Afghanistan in 2008, and Help for Heroes' Louise Watson of the RAF. My first experience of bobsleigh was in a two-man sled, but Matt started on skeleton, which he has stuck to ever since with great success.

Before we were allowed down the track, we first had to walk it. This is something that every competitor does before starting a slide (as travelling down the track is known), and is akin to horse eventers walking the course before competing. As in eventing, the purpose of the walk is to gain an understanding of the track, work out the optimum way to enter and travel through each corner, and the points at which to steer. Simply put, the fastest way to travel down a track is on the straightest line, with the bare minimum of steering. In fact, the more you steer, the slower you go, and the greater the chance of creating an uncontrollable slewing or weaving motion with your sled, known as a wave, that often results in a crash. In bobsleigh, when it comes to steering less is more. Sarah Monk, our Canadian coach, explained that there are two types of mono-bobsleigh pilots: the mechanical pilots, who work out a plan for the slide and stick to it; and the flexible pilots, who go with the flow. Both could be winners, but which would I be, I wondered?

My first track walk was with Sarah, with whom I had immediately hit it off, not least because she was kind and big hearted; she also had enormous experience of the Calgary track. For my first slide, which was to start from half-way up at Damen (the women's start), my brakeman was another Canadian, Mike Kwik. He had been to Barbados, knew many of the people I knew there, and we developed an instant rapport. Brakemen aren't allowed to use the brakes during a run, only once over the finishing line, so their job is to count the corners. On the Calgary track there are fourteen.

To say that I was anxious, as I climbed into the pilot's seat to queue up for the start at Damen, would be to minimise my feelings. I was, in fact, cooking off in my head and was close to panic. How fast would we be going? What would happen if we crashed? As so often before, I took a deep breath, and the next thing I knew we were on the track. Rather like parachuting, the sensation I felt on that first slide was high anxiety, which turned to huge exhilaration as we sped around the corners. By the time we stopped, I couldn't wait to get back to the start for another slide.

Over the course of the week that followed, I progressed higher up the track. It was soon clear to me and Sarah that for reasons neither of us fully understood, I was a natural. It also quickly became apparent to her that I was a flexible pilot, who had no problem adapting a planned slide according to circumstance. Yes, I always had a Plan A, but I could modify it in mid-slide if necessary. I was also responding to advice. I took considerable pride in all of this, but pride comes before a fall. On either my eighth or ninth start, this time from Herren (the men's start), and with a lady called Mercedes Miller as my brakeman, disaster struck. The top half of the track went well. But at Corner 8, about which Sarah had given me very specific guidance, I thought that I knew better, and the sled crashed and immediately flipped over. The next corner was very abrupt, and although crouched well down, I smacked my helmet on the wall. I was knocked out and Mercedes was thrown clear.

The next thing I knew, someone was tapping on my helmet. In short order, I was loaded into an ambulance, given a shot of morphine, and rushed to hospital. When not puking from my allergy to the painkiller, I was given a CT scan and put through the full concussion protocol. Later that day, I was discharged and taken back to the hotel. Then we all went out to a bar. Soon to be an extremely special person in my life, Mercedes turned up with her arm in a sling; she had dislocated her shoulder in the crash.

The following day, I watched other guys on the track, before it was time to head for the airport. Once back in England, I was ordered to take three weeks off, keep away from bright lights, and at the end of that time undergo a full medical. Before I knew it, it was Christmas followed by a second bobsleigh training camp at Igls in Austria, during the first week of January 2014. To be frank, as I took my seat on the flight to Innsbruck, I wasn't at all sure that I wanted to slide and, anyway, I had to undergo a medical in Austria before I would be allowed near the track.

That medical became an adventure in itself. Louise Watson took me to see a doctor in the town. On the way there, I became an object of considerable curiosity to the Tyrolean girls, who probably hadn't seen a black man before. One even pinched my bum. The medical went off without a hitch and I was cleared to slide. But I still wasn't at all sure I wanted to, particularly as there were no two-man bobsleighs in Igls and I would be making my first slide after the crash in a mono.

The following day, I did the track walk, made my way back to Damen, and climbed into the sled. I knew from my time at Knightsbridge that riders can lose their nerve after a bad fall, and the only way to avoid this was to get straight back into the saddle and take the jump again. Because of my concussion, I hadn't been allowed to do that in Calgary. Judging from the symptoms that I started to suffer as I sat in the sled, I was now reaping the consequences. My pulse rate was rising, I was sweating profusely inside my helmet, and as I got closer to the start line, I started hyper-ventilating. One of the coaches noticed this, but instead of pulling me out, he said: 'You'll be OK'. Seconds later I was pushed off. I suspect that Dicky Waygood, the Household Cavalry's Riding Master, would have approved of his action. And? Well, quite how it happened, I don't know, but as the sled gained speed I was instinctively straight back in the groove. The rest of the week passed off without incident and I finished second in the final race.

The next stop on my para-bobsleigh journey was the Paralympic Games at Sochi in Russia, in March 2014. As the sport had not been admitted to the Games, I wasn't competing; but H4H paid for me to attend for the multi-sport experience. I loved every minute of that week. Sochi was a beautiful place, the Russians couldn't have been friendlier, the local culture was interesting, the food was fantastic, and the vodka better than any that I'd ever tasted before.

On my return from Russia, I got back into my training routine, focussing particularly on strength and body-conditioning. I also heard that the first official para bobsleigh race of the 2014-15 competitive season would be for the World Cup, it would be held in Igls and that, in order to compete then and in future competitive seasons, I would have to undergo a licensing regime. This involved tests for cognitive ability, hand-eye co-ordination, and mental and physical fitness. However, because para bobsleigh was not an official Paralympic sport, I would receive no funds from UK Sport. The Household Cavalry Foundation, Help for Heroes, Blesma, and Rupert Fryer (about whom more in a moment) stepped in with funding.

In no time at all, or so it seemed, it was November 2014 and I was back in Calgary for pre-season training, with Sarah Monk once again as my coach. As there were no mono sleds in Canada at that time, I piloted a two-man sled, with Jason Sturm acting as my brakeman. A Yank by birth, Jason was serving in the US Army when he was badly injured on exercise, as a result of accidental friendly fire. Despite sustaining severe injuries to his left leg, later resulting in amputation, Jason gave medical assistance to his other comrades wounded in the same incident, thereby saving their lives. As heroes go, they don't get much more heroic than my new brakeman in Calgary. Another new face on the scene was Nicola Minichiello, a British Bobsleigh World Champion and the IBSF's representative at the training camp. She gave me the news that towards the end of the week Jason and I would be trialling the new Bo-Dyn sled then in development, which could be used either as a mono or a two-man sled.

Although I was apprehensive at the thought of tackling the Calgary track for the first time since I had crashed there the previous season, I slid well all week and worked my way up to Herren, from where I would test the Bo-Dyn with Jason. Before the slide, we all met to discuss the trial. Nicola asked me point blank if I was OK with it. Lying, I said that I was – although actually I was shitting myself. 'So tell me which way the corners go, and how you are going to tackle them,' she demanded. My mind went a complete blank. I simply couldn't remember. 'In that case you are not sliding now,' she said firmly, 'but here's what you can do. Walk the track again with Sarah and tell me how you feel in the morning.'

So, I walked the track again, re-memorized the corners from Herren, and the next day told Nicola that I was good to go. Nonetheless, I was still very nervous. Jason, who was going to push me using only one leg, sensed my anxiety: 'I know what happened last time you started from here, buddy,' he said, 'but don't worry. I trust you and I believe in you. All you have to do is believe in yourself. Ready?' I said I was, and he pushed me off. The slide was fantastic, and we celebrated afterwards with beers and steaks.

After Christmas with my family in Swindon, I headed off for Igls. I was to take over a new sled and be the official British competitor in mono, at the first of two races for the first-ever Para Bobsleigh World Cup. Matt Richardson was representing Great Britain in the skeleton. We were competing against pilots from Latvia, Germany, Austria, Canada, and the USA, in the person of Jason. At the initial captains' briefing, we were shown the trophies for which we would be competing, and I don't mind admitting that it was love at first sight. I wanted one more badly than I had ever wanted any sporting trophy before. 'You'll have to work hard for these,' we were told. 'Hard?' I thought. 'I'll bust my arse off to get one.' We were then briefed on the programme for the week, which involved three practice slides a day for the first three days, followed by two heats for the first race of the World Cup. During those three days of practice, I was regularly in the top five fastest slides.

The preparation of our sleds was vital, and the most important operation was to get a very high shine on the sled's runners in order to optimise their performance on the ice. To do this takes time, patience, skill and sandpaper. My experience of cleaning State kit at Knightsbridge was definitely a help, and I was able to pass on some tricks of the trade to the other competitors. This was because, while I wanted more than anything else to win, in para bobsleigh there is a real camaraderie amongst the competitors. We all look out for each other, our problems are shared by all, and the personal relationships we develop while competing have actually become more important than the competitions.

Regarding the rules and regulations, competitors with prosthetics have to take them off before a race and strap in, like the pilots with spinal injuries. So checking the straps was very important. In fact, I had only slid without my legs once before the heats, but thankfully found that it wasn't a problem. Another rule is that the maximum weight in a mono sled is 100 kilos. The heavier the sled, the faster it travels on the track. So we all added additional ballast to make up the difference between our body weight and the weight limit.

Finally, the race officials use either a manual or an electronic ballot to allocate the sleds, which are numbered from 1 to 20, and sled No 1 goes first. The starting position is important, because the track changes through use and weather conditions. A draw in the first five is usually the best, although it differs from track to track. At St Moritz, the fastest track in the world, it's better to be in the middle of the draw, because the track gets faster as the sun gets onto it. Another level playing field feature is that the second heat of a two-slide competition is run in the reverse order of the times achieved on the first slide; so the slowest goes first and benefits from the spritzing, or refreshing of the track, which takes place after the first heat. The draw for the sled can be even more important, as you can't use your own and so are stuck with whichever one you draw. That said, each competitor has forty minutes in the Parc Fermée after the draw to prepare the sleds, including giving the runners a final polish.

At the first race of the 2014-15 Para Bobsleigh World Cup competition, I was in the top five at the end of the first heat; I knew that if I stayed in a positive mindset I could win. When I did, it made history: the first ever race for the Para Bobsleigh World Cup had been won by a boy from Barbados. I'm happy to say that Jason came second.

From Igls we moved on to St Moritz for the second and final race of that season's World Cup. This turned out to be considerably less straightforward. Every track has its difficulties and St Moritz is no exception. The corner called the Horseshoe, the third after Monty's Bolt (the Damen start), is notoriously difficult. I was in the lead after the first heat, with Jason right behind me in second place. However, before the second heat we were allocated different sleds, and I was given one with a major problem. As a result, I came eighth in the second heat. I was completely gutted, but was told I couldn't lodge a protest, even though I wasn't planning to.

So the 2014-15 Para Bobsleigh World Cup was won by Jason and I came in second. Worse still, what I regarded as a completely unfair decision to change the sled had been made on the *actual* anniversary of the day that I lost my legs. Faced with being robbed of the World Cup, I had a choice: I could either descend into darkness or put the incident behind me, comforted by the knowledge that I was second in the world ranking. I decided to forget it and move on.

In the months that followed, I continued to train hard with Anna Greco at the gym. Together we addressed the problems I had faced during the previous bobsleigh season. The first of these was my struggle with both fitness and weight retention, and the second was my mental well-being. Since I met Anna in 2014, she and her partner and fellow instructor David

Long had quickly become important features in my life. Before I met her, I knew that I needed a fitness coach who would give me more than just physical training. I wanted someone who *understood* me, and would therefore understand the need to develop my mental fitness as well. In Anna I found the perfect person. In all the time I have known her, she has never been less than honest with me, which is something on which I can't set a value. Together we have addressed, and continue to deal with, the issues facing an elite disabled athlete. Anna and David have become part of my family. At their CrossFit gym in Cirencester, I feel that I am once again in a Troop. It's a great feeling.

At the end of the 2014-15 season, and thanks to Jason Sturm, I took up an invitation from the US military to train with them on the track at Lake Placid in New York State. Instead of flying straight there, I flew to Dulles Airport in Washington, DC, where I was met by Jason and taken to stay with his family. I quickly discovered that his wife cooked the best steaks in the world, I got a taste for Dunkin' donuts, I saw some of the country, and I even went to a basketball game. Eventually, after driving for fourteen hours, including navigating our way through a blizzard, we rocked up at Lake Placid. Once again, I found myself faced with two-man sleds only. Jason and I decided to take it in turn to brake for each other on what proved to be a very busy (i.e. difficult) track. Corner 18 was particularly hazardous, being Lake Placid's answer to Horse Shoe in St Moritz.

Nonetheless, it was all great fun and despite the difficulties of the track, during the course of the week we edged our way up to Start 3 (the equivalent of Herren at Calgary) and even managed not to crash. Until, that is, on the second-to-last day, when I was acting as Jason's brakeman for the last slide. At the notorious Corner 18 our luck ran out. In the crash that followed, I dislocated my right shoulder. Fortunately, the man who pulled me out of the sled grabbed my right arm, and without meaning to, wrenched the shoulder back into place. I was sore, and my back turned a shade of purple that I have never seen before or since on a black man. But I was alright and not in need of the casualty department at the local hospital. Later that day

I got a message from Sarah Monk: 'That will teach you not to be a brakeman. You are a PILOT!'

My next bobsleigh destination was Calgary for the start of the 2015-16 season and the first of the World Cup races. All the familiar faces from the previous year were there, including Matt and Jason. I did well in the practice slides, but ended in sixth place in the first race. I was definitely *not* satisfied with my performance, particularly as I knew that I had been expected to do much better. From Calgary we moved to Park City, a resort due east of Salt Lake City in Utah, where the second and last races of that year's World Cup were being held. Although the area is spectacular, and Park City is a wonderful place to visit, I absolutely hated the track. The result was that I came third and fifth in the two races, and was well out of contention for the World Cup.

However, while I was in Park City, I developed a friendship with Lonnie Bissonnette, a fifty-something para bobsledder from St Catherines in Ontario, who had a spinal injury that confines him to a wheel chair. Although I knew him from Calgary, it was at Park City that we really bonded. Since then, Lonnie has seen the best and the worst of me. He has taught me many life lessons and has stuck with me when, on more than one occasion, the going has got rough. It's no exaggeration to say that he has become like a brother to me.

In the wake of the disappointment of Park City, I asked H4H if I could stay in North America and move to Calgary, where Sarah Monk had invited me to train with Dennis Marineau, the head coach of Alberta Bobsleigh and the best in the sport. It is said of Dennis that when he talks, you shut up and listen. The extension was agreed, and despite some personal short-term difficulties, with which I was greatly helped by Lonnie, the training with able-bodied bobsledders was amazing. I even learned to run and jump into a sled, although this is prohibited in official para bobsleigh races. I told Lonnie, Sarah and Dennis that I wanted – no, I needed – an extended period of training in North America if I was to reach my full potential. This request resulted in me being offered the chance to live in

Canada for four to five months, from the autumn of 2016, and to join Alberta Bobsleigh alongside able-bodied pilots. I was even offered the chance of moving to Canada and joining the Alberta Police. But that would have meant living there for three years to get the necessary papers, and I wasn't prepared to be away from my family for that long.

At the start of the new year, I moved back onto the European circuit, where I won two races at Igls and one at St Moritz. This meant that I ended the 2015-16 season once again in second place in the world ranking. Back in Swindon, I was asked to be part of a Royal British Legion (RBL) campaign, which involved a lengthy photographic session and inclusion in their 100th Anniversary of the Battle of the Somme Commemorations. At about the same time, I was also invited to join H4H's High Performance Academy, set up to provide equipment and other funding for potential world-class para-athletes.

However, even with this support, it was clear to me that I would need additional funding for my pre-season training in Calgary and the 2016-17 World Cup season itself. I turned once again to the Household Cavalry Foundation, Blesma and Rupert Fryer. Given my new role with them, I also asked the RBL for their financial support and was somewhat dismayed (to say the least) when I discovered that, without telling me, they had taken my request to H4H. This created a shedload of difficulties and recriminations with H4H that I could well have done without. Fortunately, an all-party meeting sorted out the mess, and my training budget was agreed and funded.

On the subject of financial support, Rupert Fryer is a former Blues and Royals officer who has built a very successful career in private banking in Switzerland, where he is a director of Bank J. Safra Sarasin based in Geneva. He left the Regiment long before I joined, and I don't know how I came to his attention. It was probably through the HCF or its predecessor organisation, the Household Cavalry Operational Casualties Fund (HCOCF), which was set up by amongst others my co-author. If Lonnie Bissonnette is like a brother to me, then Rupert has become a second father. Not only has he been immensely supportive of me financially, but equally importantly, he has given me huge emotional support. From the start of our friendship, when he told me that he had heard my story and wanted to help, he and his wife have watched all my races in St Moritz. He also stays in touch with me by telephone and email, and whenever we are both in the UK, we meet up in London. I am blessed to know him.

With everything in place, I flew back to Calgary in November 2016. There I met up with Lonnie for pre-season training with a new coach, Tom Samuel, who trained the Jamaican able-bodied bobsleigh team. The upcoming season was the largest yet, with World Cup races in Calgary, Park City, Oberhof (Germany), Igls and St Moritz. Despite my time under Tom's wing, the season did not go well and I ended the season ranked fifth. Clearly something had gone wrong and I needed to rethink my whole strategy. Back in England, I discussed the problem with Anna Greco, who for reasons completely unconnected with her, I had not used for the pre-season fitness workouts. We decided that I should go back to scratch with both my physical and mental training.

By the time I returned to Calgary in November 2017, I had a whole new attitude to the sport and myself. The track training was really tough, in temperatures that were often around minus-forty degrees. This may have contributed to a change in attitude towards us by the able-bodied pilots, with whom we were sharing the track. I now felt that they regarded us as serious bobsleigh athletes. At first, I didn't produce outstanding results, coming fifth in both World Cup races on the Calgary track. My disappointment at this poor performance was offset somewhat with the news that H4H, Blesma and HCF would be providing me with my own sled for training the following year.

From Calgary, Lonnie and I flew to Montreal, where we hired a car and drove to Lake Placid. I arrived there feeling quite apprehensive. I had to up my game if I was to do well in the World Cup – and I did, coming first and second in the two races there. I returned home for Christmas in really good spirits and in close contention with Lonnie for the title, which would be decided on the European tracks. At the next races at Igls and Oberhof, I came first in all four. However, by the time we got to St Moritz, the pressure was starting to get to me, and I only achieved a second and a fifth. Nevertheless, I won the 2017-18 Para Bobsleigh World Cup. Result! Later, at Lillehammer, where I competed in the Para Bobsleigh World Championship races, sadly I only came eighth.

By the start of the 2018-19 season, I had my own sled. Somewhat unexpectedly, as I had not asked for one, Blesma also provided a manager, who was to act as my interface with the charities and make all my admin arrangements. First, I had to get the sled to Canada for the pre-season track training, and the airfreight was not cheap. To my huge relief, Blesma once again stepped in with funding and I arrived in Calgary with my sled, Lonnie, and a plan of action. It's an old Army saying that no plan survives the first encounter with the enemy, and in my case the opposition came in the form of horrible weather. Lonnie and I were happy to slide in temperatures that plunged below minus-forty degrees, but it was a very hard ask of the coaches, who nonetheless remained very supportive.

As a consequence of the bad weather, we had a lot of unplanned leisure time. This may have been the reason why the season didn't start well for me. I achieved only a fifth and a seventh place in the opening World Cup races at Calgary. Worse was to come at Park City, my least favourite track in the world, where I had two bad races. By the end of 2018, it looked as though I had no hope of repeating my World Cup success of the previous year. However, the Caribbean-style Christmas dinners in Swindon were followed in January 2019 by two good races at Oberhof, where I came third twice. I was placed again at Lillehammer, where I also achieved third in the first ever European Championship; and thanks to a good performance at St Moritz, I ended the season in third place for the World Cup. I then had to race back to Lake Placid for that season's four-heat World Championship, in which I came second. Overall, it wasn't a bad year; but I hadn't won, and that meant a lot to me.

I began the 2019-20 season in great physical and mental shape, thanks to Anna and David. However, it didn't start well. This was not because of the weather or my performance, but because the Calgary track was closed and Covid-19 was lurking on the horizon. Instead of heading for Canada for pre-season training, I went straight to Europe for the first of the World Cup races at Lillehammer, where things started to look up and I achieved a first and a second there. Then at Oberhof I scored two firsts, and in St Moritz a fourth and a first. By the start of 2020, I was on a high, even though the World Championship had been cancelled due to the virus. I headed for Lake Placid in a really good state, and with a healthy lead of eighty points ahead of Lonnie in the World Cup. Unfortunately, this was not to last.

While we were in St Moritz, Lonnie and I had agreed that we would rent a house in Lake Placid. There, despite taking precautions, I caught a cold, which put me in a very difficult mood. Then a real disaster struck. On the way up the track, one of the sleds fell off its transport and was damaged. For some reason, I was sure that I would be allocated this sled – and I was. Inevitably, I crashed on the first practice slide. I wasn't badly hurt and I said nothing, although I had bruised my neck. But the combination of that and my cold meant that I had a horrible week of training. However, everything was put back into perspective for me when we got the news that Lonnie's sister had died.

Despite all this gloom, things improved with the opening race, in which I came fourth. My time in the opening heat of the second race was worse, and I came sixth. But because of the way that the points scoring system worked for the Para Bobsleigh World Cup, I was still top of the leader board at the start of the second heat of the final race at Lake Placid – and I knew how I could improve my time. Then, before I could slide, something truly awful happened.

One of the early starters in that second heat at Lake Placid was Ziva Lavrinc, a Slovenian lady who is a paraplegic. Outside the hut at the top of the run a blizzard was raging; inside, we watched Ziva's run on a TV monitor. At Corner 4 she had a horrible crash, was knocked unconscious, and then hurtled down the rest of the track. We all felt absolutely awful about this. Ziva's crash, the deteriorating track conditions, and the fact that, as the blizzard closed in, it was becoming almost impossible to get the sleds back to the top of the track, led to the officials stopping the race. This left me in first place for the World Cup. But my lead over Lonnie had been reduced to twenty points, an uncomfortably close margin, and the next race was at my nemesis, Park City. We travelled there via Lonnie's home at St Catherines, so that we could attend his sister's funeral. Consequently, although I held a narrow lead for the World Cup, my head was not in a good place when we arrived at Park City for the last races of the season.

The first news we were given at the captains' briefing was that we were to share sleds with a women's mono bobsleigh group. Inevitably, such is my luck, I ended up sharing a sled with a lady who was new to the sport. Equally inevitably, she broke the sled's axle on the first day of training. 'How much worse can this it get?' I thought. The answer is that I achieved my worst races ever in a World Cup, coming tenth and twelfth. This eliminated my points lead, and I slipped into second place behind Lonnie, although I had secured the European Championship. When I was called to take my place on the podium, unintentionally I didn't shake the other competitors' hands, which was really bad sportsmanship on my part; I immediately regretted it and apologised. I can only say, by way of an excuse, that my head was in a really bad place. Taken in the round, it had been a not unsuccessful season, but I left the USA on a real low. Even though I was the European Champion, and known respectfully by my fellow competitors as 'Black Ice', I was determined not to touch the sport ever again.

Time and friends, however, are great healers. Thanks to the support of my family, the Wiltshire Police, and the encouragement and skills of Anna and David, I did regain my hunger for bobsleigh, although the 2020–21 season did not start well for me. Because of Covid-19, the races for the World Championship, World Cup and European Championship were limited in number and venues, and pre-competition travel was severely restricted. Unlike the competitors who lived in the mountains, I was unable to get in any training before the World Championship heats in St Moritz. Worse still, two weeks before I was due to leave for Switzerland I was hospitalised in Swindon for a few days with a painful bacterial infection in my gut. Nonetheless, I managed to come fourth in the World Championship, behind a Swiss, a Canadian and a Swede. Ten days later, I won Bronze Medals on both the second and third days of the World Cup at La Plagne in France, ending up fifth overall; and I achieved the Silver Medal in the European Championship, finishing a cumulative 0.02 seconds behind the winner.

My sights are now firmly set on winning the next Para Bobsleigh World and European Championships and the World Cup, and also winning Gold for Great Britain just as soon as para bobsleigh is admitted to the Paralympics. In the meantime, I will continue to train for the sport, work for the police and reflect on life, death and the whole black thing.

CHAPTER 12

Life, Death and the Whole Black Thing

IN MY EXPERIENCE there is nothing that so focuses one's approach to life as coming face-to-face with death. I don't just mean being in a life-threatening situation, but actually being in the presence of Death himself. Between the IED explosion that blew off my legs and waking up in Selly Oak, I had a strange experience that became the background to my outlook on life, which is the subject of this final chapter.

At the time, as far as the world was concerned, I was in intensive care, drugged up to the eyeballs and out-for-the-count. However, as far I was concerned, I knew that I was lying on my bed in my tent at Musa Qala and that there was nothing wrong with me. Then, without warning, my body started dropping through the mattress and the earth beneath it. As I sank downwards, for some reason I kept repeating and repeating: 'Please, God, don't take me – I'm not ready.' The next thing that I knew, I was standing in the courtyard of a house, which looked rather like the sort of places in the Bible that I had heard about in Sunday school. To my left was a door with a flaming torch on either side of it, and to my right was corridor. Before I could decide which way to go, I ended up back on my bed.

I had this experience not once but several times. It was only on the last occasion that I didn't immediately return to my bed. Instead, standing in the sandy courtyard, I knew that I had to choose either the door or the corridor. For some reason, I chose the corridor and started to walk down it. As I did so, it seemed to stretch out in front of me. I kept on walking, and at last I saw an opening with a light, which was drawing closer and getting larger all the time. Suddenly, I heard a deep voice with a Barbadian accent: 'I am not ready for you, yet.' My body immediately returned to my bed, where I found myself surrounded, horrifyingly, by fanged demons. The next thing I remembered was waking up in a hospital bed at Selly Oak, and my boots were killing me.

I know that it's easy to rationalise away this story as something dreamt up by my subconscious mind during a drug-induced coma. But I *know* that the experience was real. I was dying: that is a fact. As my mum had prayed when she asked Him for me, I begged God that I be spared death. I was spared: that is also a fact. What I don't know is the reason why He spared me. However, I firmly *believe* that I was given a second chance, so I could do something with my life. It has taken me time to work out what that could be, but I am now certain that it has two main purposes.

The first is to use my second chance at life as a way of thanking all those people who saved me, nursed me back to health, helped rehabilitate me, and then gave me the physical, moral, financial and psychological support that I needed and still need. These wonderful people include the military and civilian doctors and nurses who treated me; the experts at Headley Court who rehabilitated me; and all the charities and, more particularly, Rupert Fryer and the Household Cavalry, who have supported me *and* my family in every conceivable way and still do. There are also the individuals, both in the military and in civvy street, who have encouraged me; and not forgetting the taxpayers who have supported me financially.

Given what had happened to me, I could easily have banked my pension and basked in the sympathy of friends and strangers. I could have become a recluse, or even in despair at my disability, taken my own life, as some of my comrades have tragically done. I would have had every right to do any of those things, having lost my legs in the service of my Queen and country. But I felt then and I feel now, that to have sat back and done nothing would have shown great ingratitude to all those who helped me. Worse still, it would have been to waste my second chance. I would be merely existing, and when I come to the final reckoning, my life would have had no purpose whatsoever. In fact, I might as well have died after the IED struck my vehicle.

So I have set myself new goals, starting with making a success of my new career with the Wiltshire Police. A lot of people have asked me why I have gone back into the law-enforcement business, sixteen years after I handed in my badge in Bridgetown. The answer is that I thought it was time to figure out who I was *without* sport, particularly as I realised I was starting to rely on it. That does not mean that I am about to drop bobsleigh. Quite the reverse, for I have set my medium-term goals in the sport. Beyond that, I want to coach both our able-bodied and para-athlete bobsleigh national teams. Why? Because not only do I need to give something back to bobsleigh, by encouraging people into it, but also because, as a disabled athlete, I really understand the challenges in a way that even the best able-bodied coach can't. How am I able to plan to do all of these things? Because the Wiltshire Police makes the time available to elite athletes to train and compete. I also plan to get my private pilot's licence. But more important than any of that, I am going to be the best father that I can to my three daughters.

I believe that the second reason I was spared is to use my past achievements, and those future goals, to convince Caribbean and other kids of colour that there are *no limits*. You see – and I'm now talking *directly* to those kids who are tempted by the gangs, the drugs and the apparently easy life of crime – it doesn't matter if you leave school without any qualifications, as I did, providing you have a dream and you then pursue it.

Sure, between you and that dream are barriers, but they are made of glass. They don't obscure your goal, nor do they prevent you achieving it, because with determination you can break through them. Yes, you might get some cuts and bruises; you might even lose a limb or two, but so what? Nothing worth having in life comes easy. And, as I'm sloganizing, it was the great American President, Franklin D Roosevelt, who said that there is nothing to fear except fear itself. My take on that is that the only person who can label you as a failure is yourself. If you have a dream, the only person who can stop you making it reality is you, and the only way that you fail is if you quit – or if you choose not to start at all.

As long as you live, you can be something great. But you must give yourself the chance, and to do that you have to change your mental attitude. If you surround yourself with negativity, you can't succeed. You need to block out those who say you can't win because of who you are, or because of the colour of your skin. Instead, you must listen only to people who have a positive attitude and who encourage you to be the best version of yourself. Yeah, yeah, I hear you mutter; it's easy for you to say that. But is it? I'm no different as to race, colour, background and education to the thousands of you who opt out. I haven't used the excuse that the dice are loaded against me, particularly because of my colour, heritage and disability, and stopped trying.

Which brings me to the touchy subject of racism and anti-racist activism, and here I know that I am going to make some enemies. But what follows is based on my personal experiences. I *know* that racism can be used as an excuse for failure. I also believe that anti-racist activists harm their cause by their negative approach to the subjects of prejudice and heritage. In the current climate, almost anything that is said to a black man is taken as racist, whether or not it is meant to be.

Interpretation is everything. For example, when I was in basic training at Pirbright, absolutely everything yelled at me by our instructors could have been taken as racist, but it clearly wasn't. And despite being warned when I signed on that the Household Cavalry was the most racist unit in the British Army, the reality was completely different. Yes, as in the wider world, there were some dickheads in the Regiment who were racist, but I was never, ever subjected to racial abuse. In fact, for the entire time that I served in the Household Cavalry, I never encountered any racism or racist undertones: I was treated as a mature soldier, whose skin colour was a complete irrelevance. If I got bollocked, it was because I had messed up, not because I was black. One NCO actually told me that I had changed his perception of black people.

Another man I served with convinced himself that I had 'attitude', and consequently gave me a very hard time. After I was injured, he said, 'I know we had our differences, but I'm now really sorry at the things that passed between us.' Nonetheless, this same man (who is no longer in the Army) more recently took to Facebook and wrote that blacks need to 'get over the four hundred years of oppression bollocks and stop being victims.' I did not respond, but he later apologised to me. However, he has persisted in posting online stuff that I deeply disagree with. This is partly because he's an ignorant man, who doesn't know any different, and partly because of the way he was brought up. His current views would never have been tolerated if he had expressed them when he was in the Regiment.

Which brings me to my firmly held belief that the way out of the present situation is not negative protest but education. No one is born with a racist attitude; it is something that is learned or absorbed from the people around you. No one is born a drug dealer or a thief, but if you are brought up in that culture it will seem perfectly normal. So racial tolerance can be taught and racism can be un-taught, because racism is no different to sexism, anti-Semitism, homophobia, and all the other bad 'isms' of our age, some of which have already been dramatically reduced through education.

Of course, it is true that, amongst others, Stonewall's protests for gay rights and the MeToo movement against sexual abuse have led directly to changes in the law and ended the casting couch culture of Hollywood. But it is *education* that has made people more aware of the implications of what they are saying and doing; and it is education not protests that changes attitudes. I know because it changed mine. Barbados has still not legalised gay marriage. When I first came to England as an adult, I was horrified at the sight of men holding hands in public. However, during my time in the Household Cavalry I was taught about diversity, and now homosexuality is no longer a problem as far as I am concerned. So, although being gay is not for me, I have lots of friends who are gay. When I arrived here, having them as mates would have been unthinkable. Most importantly, I've been taught that it's not for me to judge people as anything other than either good or bad human beings.

That said, I'm not so naïve as to think for one moment that education will eliminate racism. The reality is that no matter what you do, there will always be people who you like and people who you dislike. However, we have no choice but to live together, and we will only achieve that with respect for one another. Complaining just gets people's backs up, as we can see on social media. Bob Marley really summed it up for me when he said: 'Yes, we have been oppressed; yes, there is racism; but if you get down and quarrel every day, you're saying prayers to the Devil'.

Because of the behaviour of a small minority of black men, society has labelled us as aggressive, angry and violent. This has had a direct impact on blacks' interaction with law enforcement. Unfortunately, the current anti-racist activism has further set the relationship between blacks and whites on edge, particularly with the police. Even in this country, the knee-jerk reaction now of a black person when approached by a policeman is to be on guard. How much better would it be for everyone if, in the first instance, we blacks showed respect for the law and spoke in calm tones?

I say this not because I am working in law enforcement, but because I am black. If we blacks start with respect, then if the police are in any way at fault (and the onus is always on them to behave properly), we can and should complain. But we should do it *afterwards*. A fat lot of good that did George Floyd, and others before and since, I hear you say. True. But that was in the USA and we are in the UK, where things are mostly done differently. I've been stopped for no reason by the police, once when driving back home from Gatwick Airport. I didn't react aggressively, but with respect. The policeman and I had a good chat, and I then went on my way. Should I have been stopped? Who knows? But because of the way I reacted, there were no problems. We shouldn't immediately assume the worst and set up a confrontation; all that does is re-enforce pre-conceived attitudes and prejudices. As people, whatever our colour, we should remember that for every action there is an equal and opposite reaction.

The anti-racist activists say that blacks are oppressed and are at a disad-vantage, particularly when it comes to jobs. This is a notion that I find difficult to accept when I look at my own life. I can't talk about what does or doesn't happen when it comes to the top jobs; but I can say that at my level and in my direct experience of the Army, elite sport, and the police, we all have the same opportunity to receive a decent education and then to compete for any job *on merit alone*. There may be stuff going on behind closed doors that I don't know about, but it has never stopped me achieving my goals. I firmly believe that if we are 'oppressed', it is in our minds; and if it is in our minds, then we have the power to emancipate ourselves from that mental slavery. But until we free ourselves from that state of mind – and no one else is going to do it for us – we will continue to feel that we are being oppressed.

The activists also say that whites have to change their attitude to us. I agree. But we also have to change our attitudes to whites. I believe that you reap what you sow. Well, that cuts both ways. We have flaws and have to admit our flaws. On a daily basis, we are killing our own people through senseless violence and the sale of drugs. This has to stop. We must also stop blaming history, which we can't change, and start making new history together; and we must stop taking a partial view of our past. The British may have been deeply involved in the slave trade, but the tribal chiefs in West Africa were also complicit in that trade for their own profit. White slavers didn't capture my ancestors, they bought them already enslaved by our own people. This is a fact which no one, with the recent exception of Trevor Phillips, now dares to mention.

Then we must never forget that it was white British politicians who abolished the slave trade within the British Empire, and it was a white British General, Charles Gordon, who supressed the Arab-run slave trade in East Africa and then died defending black Christians against the slave-owning Mahdists. And it was a white British government that gave permission to the mixed-race Jamaican, Mary Seacole, to set up a rest home for British officers in the Crimea, and those same white officers who allowed her onto the battlefield to tend the wounded.

These, and many other facts, are uncomfortable for the anti-racist activists. Yes, unjust and immoral things have happened to us blacks, even in the very recent past, of which the Windrush scandal is but one. Some of my uncles came to England on the MV *Empire Windrush* to help rebuild this country after the Second World War. Nobody forced them to come. They came willingly to help and they believed that, in return, they would be rewarded with a better life in their new home. The bureaucratic mistakes made seventy years later, leading to their dreams being turned into nightmares, should be treated by both communities not as evidence of racism but as a lesson in how, even in the enlightened twenty-first century, things can go horribly wrong. Instead of apportioning blame and holding up such awful incidents as yet more evidence of prejudice and oppression, we should work together to look for solutions so that it can't happen again.

Better still, let's stop preaching hate and start teaching that we are one human race, marooned on a tiny planet hurtling through space. We must teach *every* kid that colour, creed, sexuality, and all the other things that differentiate us, are also the things that bring us together as human beings. We must also teach our kids that the world is their oyster and that they should seize life with both hands, set themselves a goal, push through the barriers that will inevitably be erected in their path, and then march with determination towards it. That's what I'm doing, and I'm doing it without any qualifications or my own legs.

In closing this book, I want to send my last thoughts to someone who resembles my early self. I don't know his (or it may be her) name, but I send this message to him in the hope that my story, my ambitions, my thoughts about life, death and the whole black thing, and my beliefs and sometimes controversial opinions, might make a difference, even if it's only to him. Although he doesn't have a name, I know he, and many other boys and girls like him, exists because I was him. My message is this:

> You may not achieve all your dreams, as I may not achieve all of mine. But if
> – when you get to the light at the end of your tunnel – you can say that you
> have given it your best shot, you will have had a more fulfilling life than if
> you hadn't – and God will welcome you. Don't exist, LIVE!

And finally …

This book was conceived and written, in its entirety, during the Covid-19 crisis of 2020. We (the co-authors), who had never met before the project started, did not actually meet face-to-face until after the manuscript had been finished. This curious state-of-affairs was partly due to the first nation-wide lockdown of 2020 and partly due to the fact that, in mid-August 2020, while maintaining his daily fitness workouts at CrossFit, Corie started his training to become a Police Community Support Officer (PCSO) with the Wiltshire Police. This left him with little time for anything else, and it is remarkable that he found the time for this book.

Again because of Covid-19, Corie's police training, which he completed in November 2020, was carried out remotely. But, as he says, this was made easy for him by the Wiltshire Police: 'Not only did they bend over backwards to make me comfortable in every possible way, but they have also treated me as one of their own since the day that I started training. Better even than that, Wiltshire Police gave me all the tools that I needed to complete my training, and even told me in advance that my first posting as a PCSO would be to Central South. I am now looking forward to the opportunity of starting the training to become a Police Constable next year.'

CORIE MAPP

CHRISTOPHER JOLL

GLOSSARY
Army slang, Abbreviations, Household Cavalry Ranks and Other Mysteries

ACOG Advanced Combat Optical Gunsight

Angel Flight Helicopter recovery of dead British servicemen

ATO Royal Engineers Ammunition Technical Officer, usually bomb disposal

ATR Army Training Regiment

Back trooped Made to do the training course again

Bajan A citizen of Barbados

Banter Light-hearted and humorous exchanges, often 'black', frequently profane, scatological or irreverent and always liberally spiced with obscenities

Battle Back An adaptive sport and adventurous training programme. It was established by the Royal British Legion in 2011 to support wounded, injured and sick armed services personnel. More recently the service has been expanded to introduce wellbeing courses for veterans

Battle Group An all-arms operational/combat formation in the field, formed around either an infantry or an armoured unit and commanded by a Lieutenant Colonel

BATUS British Army Training Unit Suffield, Canada

BDF Barbados Defence Force

Beasted In this context: pushed to the limit and, sometimes, beyond

BGPD Barbados Government Printing Department

Binned Thrown off a horse

Bimshire Barbados

Bivvy A makeshift tent, usually attached to the side of an armoured vehicle

Bivvy bag A waterproof sleeping bag

Blacks The black horses, usually Irish, used by the Household Cavalry

Blesma The charity that supports limbless serving and ex-servicemen and women

Bluey Forces airletter

Bob, bob-up Polishing kit

Bollocking Severe verbal reprimand, usually including expletives

Bombardier Royal Artillery rank equivalent to a Corporal

BPA British Paralympic Association

Brew Hot drink, usually tea

Brewed-up Tea making – also when a military vehicle is his by an explosive device or round

Bright chain A steel chain that is worn around a cavalry horse's neck and connected to the underside of the bridle. It was originally designed to prevent sword cuts to the horse's neck

Brimstone Royal Engineers mine and IED clearance team

BYS Barbados Youth Service

Casevac Casualty evacuation

CB Companion of the Most Honourable Order of the Bath

CBE Commander of the Most Excellent Order of the British Empire

CFB Canadian Forces Base, Suffield, Canada

CFT Combat Fitness Test

CGC Conspicuous Gallantry Cross

Chinook Twin-rotor heavy lift and casualty evacuation helicopter

Civvies Civilians or civilian clothes, depending on the context

Closed down Term used when the driver of a military vehicle, usually a tank, closes the armoured hatch above him and drives using only a unity vision periscope

CO Commanding Officer, always referred to in the Household Cavalry as 'the Colonel' or 'Colonel [first name]'

Co-ax Machine gun co-axially mounted with the main armament of a tank or armoured car

Combermere Combermere Barracks, Windsor

CoH Corporal of Horse, Household Cavalry rank equivalent to Sergeant

CSM Company Sergeant Major (WO2)

Cuirasses Polished steel breast & back plates worn by both Regiments of the Household Cavalry in Full Dress

CVO Casualty Visiting Officer

CVR(T) Combat Vehicle Reconnaissance (Tracked)

Damen Women's start on a bobsleigh track

DFC Distinguished Flying Cross

Dickers Taliban target spotters

DL Deputy Lieutenant

DMRC Defence Medical Rehabilitation Centre

Donkey Walloper Nickname used by the rest of the Army when referring to the Household Cavalry

Dragon gun 105mm L118 Light Gun

DSO Distinguished Service Order

Dutyman Household Cavalry soldier on ceremonial duty

ERI Exercise Rehabilitation Instructor

Five-footed A horse that appears to have one too many legs when jumping, resulting in a very jerky experience for the rider

FLET Forward Line of Enemy Troops

FOB Forward Operating Base, a logistics centre

GCB Knight Grand Cross of the Most Honourable Order of the Bath

GCVO Knight Grand Cross of the Royal Victorian Order

G-force Gravitational pull

Get go Start

GPMG 7.62 mm General Purpose Machine Gun

Gunners Royal Regiment of Artillery

H4H Help for Heroes

HCF Household Cavalry Foundation, a charitable trust established to support serving and former members of the Household Cavalry, and their families, across a wide range of activities

HCMR Household Cavalry Mounted Regiment, the Household Cavalry's ceremonial duties formation

HCOCF Household Cavalry Operational Casualties Fund

HCR Household Cavalry Regiment, the Household Cavalry's operational formation

HE High Explosive

Herren Men's start on a bobsleigh track

HLS Helicopter Landing Site

IBSF International Bobsleigh and Skeleton Federation

ICU Intensive Care Unit

Icom chatter Taliban radio traffic

IED Improvised Explosive Device

ISAF NATO's International Security Assistance Force in Afghanistan

Jack boots Thigh-high black boots worn by officers and men of the Household Cavalry in Full Dress

Jackal A four-wheeled, open-topped armoured vehicle armed with a 0.50-inch Browning Machine Gun

KCMG Knight Commander of the Most Distinguished Order of St Michael and St George

Kick-off Enemy action

Kinetic High activity military zone

Knightsbridge The colloquial name for Hyde Park Barracks

LCoH Lance Corporal of Horse, Household rank equivalent to a Corporal

LCpl Lance Corporal

Lance Jack Army slang for a Lance Corporal

Leaguer Military vehicle camp in the field

MBE Member of the Most Excellent Order of the British Empire

MC Military Cross

MERT Medical Emergency Response Team, usually helicopter-borne

MIST report Mechanism, Type, Signs, Treatment – an operational medical report

Mucking out Cleaning the horses' stalls and loose boxes of soiled sbedding and replacing it with clean

MVO Member of the Royal Victorian Order

NAAFI Navy, Army and Air Force Institutes – the organisation that provides and runs shops, cafés and other leisure facilities on armed services bases

NATO North Atlantic Treaty Organisation

9-liner Medical evacuation request

NHS National Health Service

OBE Officer of the Most Excellent Order of the British Empire

Obeah woman A healer

Off the board In line for promotion

OP Observation Post

Op BARMA or BARMA 4-man regimental mine and IED clearance team

Patch Army married quarters

Pax Military Insurance A division of Towergate Insurance

PB Patrol Base

PiP Paralympic Inspiration Programme

PT Physical training

PTI Physical Training Instructor

PTSD Post Traumatic Stress Disorder

Queen's Shorthand for The Queen's Life Guard, the daily sentry/guard duty at Horse Guards, Whitehall

RAF Royal Air Force

RBL Royal British Legion

RBPF Royal Barbados Police Force

RCM Regimental Corporal Major

Regimental Corporal Major Household Cavalry rank equivalent to Regimental Sergeant Major (WO1)

Rehab Rehabilitation

REME LAD Royal Electrical and Mechanical Engineers Light Aid Detachment, technical support for an armoured or armoured reconnaissance unit at Squadron level

RHQ Regimental Headquarters

RLC Royal Logistic Corps

Rolling back Post-exercise military vehicle maintenance

Route green Safe path, cleared of mines and IEDs

RPG Rocket Propelled Grenade

RPTC Regional Police Training Centre (Barbados)

RQMC Regimental Quarter Master Corporal (Warrant Officer Class 2), equivalent to Regimental Quarter Master Sergeant

RRU Rapid Response Unit

R&R Rest and Recuperation, usually at the end of an exercise or operation

RSOI Reception, Staging, Onward Movement and Integration briefing

RV Rendezvous

Sabre Squadron Armoured fighting unit, usually three or four per Regiment

Salamander CVR(T) command vehicle, unique to BATUS

Samson or Sammy CVR(T) recovery vehicle

Sappers Corps of Royal Engineers

Scimitar CVR(T) light tank equipped with a 30 mm RARDEN cannon

SCM Squadron Corporal Major

Screen Outer defensive ring

Sliding Riding a bobsleigh track

Spotter Sniper's assistant

Squadron Corporal Major Household Cavalry rank equivalent to Company Sergeant Major (WO2)

GLOSSARY

SSU Special Services Unit

Staff Corporal Household Cavalry rank equivalent to Staff Sergeant

Stag Sentry duty

Sultan CVR(T) command vehicle

Surgeon Lieutenant Colonel Household Cavalry Regimental Medical Officer, always titled as 'Surgeon' followed by rank

Tabbed Tactical Advance to Battle

Terps Interpreters

The Tins Nickname of The Life Guards

Three-bar Corporal of Horse

Turret surfing Sitting on top of an armoured vehicle turret – a safer place to be than inside the vehicle when the threat of IEDs is greater than small arms fire

Vallon Metal detector

Vikings Royal Anglian Regiment

Yomping Marching in full kit over difficult terrain

Yorks Yorkshire Regiment

Zero(ed) Weapon sight adjustment

INDEX

ABF The Soldiers' Charity, *xi*

Abundant Life Assembly, Pentacostal Church, Saint Michael, Barbados, 7

Afghanistan, 88

Camp Bastion 81-2, 83-6, 89

MERT (Medical Emergency Reponse Team) 96

see also Helmand Province

Al Minhad Air Base, Dubai 81

Albert, Life Guards 'black' 60, 65-6

Ali, Muhammad 7

Allen, Private Mark 97

Amos, Corporal of Horse Lee 58

anti-racist activists 153-5

Army Training Centre (ATC), Pirbright 42, 43-51

1 Army Training Regiment, 59 (Asten) Battery, Sphynx Troop 44

Bader, Group Captain Sir Douglas, CBE, DSO*, DFC* 116

Badrutt's Hotel, St Moritz 132

Bailey's rum shop 9

Barbados 3-4, 152

holidays in 49, 55, 77, 114, 117-18

Barbados Cadet Corps 16-17

Barbados Defence Force (BDF) 117

Barbados Regiment 21

Cadet Reserve 21

Barbados Government Printing Department 21

Barbados Youth Service (BYS) 18, 19-20

Barrow, Errol Walton, PC, QC, Prime Minister of Barbados 11-12, 22

Baskh, Lance Corporal Tariq 51

Batson, Mr 15

BattleBack sports teams

golf 120

cricket 124

sitting volleyball 126

BATUS (British Army Training Unit Suffield), Canada 71-5

Begg, Captain Ingus 21

Belize, Life Guards 'black' 60

Bell, Jordan 'Dinger' 72, 73, 74-5, 77

Bell, Trooper Kenny 87

Ben, police dog 30-2, 34

Best, Tino 17, 20

Bissonnette, Lonnie 141, 143

black men

and anti-racist activists 153-4

and notion of oppression 153-4

change of attitude 154

Blake, Lance Corporal of Horse Sam 100, 101

Blenheim, Life Guards 'black' 60, 64

Blesma charity 121, 136, 142, 144
bobsleigh
    origins 132
    ambition to coach 150
    see also Para Bobsleigh
Bodney Camp, Norfolk, HCMR
    Summer Camp 52, 54-5
Bridgeman, Cerepha 'Tracy' 30-1, 35,
    36, 41
Bridgetown, Barbados, Central Police
    Station 26-7
British High Commission, Military
    Attaché 36-7
Brize Norton, RAF 71, 81, 84
Brooker, Lee 95-6
Brooks, Major David 58
Broom, Lance Corporal of Horse
    Jamie 53
Broome, Assistant Superintendent
    'Fancy Basket' 26
Brophy, Corporal of Horse John 83
Brown, Regimental Quarter Master
    Corporal Warren 118
Brownlee, Alistair, MBE 129
Brownlee, Jonny 129
Brummell, HE Paul 118
Buckingham Palace, first sight of 12
Bulford Camp, Wiltshire 68
Burke, Mr 15
Butah, Major Justin 86

Cadogan, PC Gregory 39-40
Cakes 4 Casualties 108
Calgary, Alberta, Canada 71, 133-5
Cameron, Rt Hon David 106
Camp Bastion, Afghanistan 81-2,
    83-6, 89

Campbell, Lieutenant (later Captain)
    Barnabas *x–xii*, 79, 99
    in Afghanistan 87, 90, 95
    visit to Selly Oak 108
    to Barbados 118
    support for CM 121
Castlemartin Camp, Pembrokeshire,
    live gunnery training 69-70, 79-80
Cave, Paul 14
Chandler, Alvin 37
Chaplin, Daniel 72, 73, 74
charities 127-8
    see also Blesma; Help for Heroes
    (H4H); Household Cavalry
    Foundation; Royal British Legion
    (RBL)
Charles II, King 45
children of colour, advice to 150-1, 155
Clarke, Commander Aquinas 40
Clarke, Fred 37, 41
Clarke, Lieutenant Commander 117
Clifton Hall, Barbados 4
Codrington High School, Barbados
    12, 13-14
Collins, Company Sergeant Major
    Iain 100, 101
Combermere Barracks, Windsor 51-2,
    68-9
    Khaki Ride training 52-5
Common Military Syllabus 43
Commonwealth War Graves, Ypres,
    Menin Gate 49
Cooper, Lance Corporal Elliot 53
COT Printery, Bridgetown 21
Covid-19 146, 156
Crewe, Colonel Tristan 120

death, in presence of 148-9

Defence Medical Rehabilitation Centre (DMRC) *see* Headley Court

Digby, police dog 30-1

Doyle, Lance Corporal Eddie 53

Driver, Captain Martin 106

Drummond, first Life Guards 'black' 52, 53, 54, 55, 60

Dukes, Corporal of Horse Bert 58, 61

'duppies' 31

Edge Cliff, Barbados 5

Elizabeth, HM The Queen 66

Empire Windrush, MV 155

European Championships, Great Britain Sitting Volleyball Team, Poland 125-6

Exercise ICEBREAKER 48

Exercise TRADE WINDS, SSU 37-8

Ferdinand, Les, MBE *vii*

Fergusson, Corporal Ricky, MC 106

Festival of Remembrance, Royal Albert Hall 65

Fitzgerald, Corporal of Horse 63

Floyd, George 153

Flynn, Regimental Corporal Major Mick, CGC, MC 68, 69

Foran, Chloe 55-6, 61

Foran, Reece 49, 51, 55-6, 61

Foster, Squadron Corporal Major 56

Francis, Lance Corporal of Horse Ruel 'Frankie' 86, 87, 90, 95, 97-8, 113
and IED explosion 97-8, 99-100
in Selly Oak 106, 108

Fryer, Rupert 121, 136, 149
financial support 142-3

Fullerton, Lieutenant Colonel Harry 88-9, 95, 116-17

Gardner, Regimental Corporal Major (RCM) Adrian 53, 88-9

Garrison Savannah Racecourse, Bridgetown 21

Garrison Secondary School, Barbados 16

Gatting, Mike 124

Gemma, Life Guards 'black' 64

Ghana, President of, State Visit (2007) 65-6

Gibbs, Captain Rob 53

Gibson, Corporal of Horse Byron 70

Gibson, Miss 12

Glendairy Prison, Barbados, riot 39-40

Glew, George 111, 112, 114

Gooding, Andrea 30

Gooding, Ucelia 30, 104

Gordon, General Charles 154

Grace, Renier 20-1, 30, 114
wedding 118

Graham, Sergeant 25

Greco, Anna 123, 139-40, 143, 144, 146

Green, PC Kevin 37-8

Griffin, Lieutenant Colonel Ralph 58

Griffith, Hudson 20

Gurkhas, in Afghanistan 86

Guthrie of Craigiebank, Field Marshal Lord 115

Habib, Helmand, Patrol Base (PB) 94-7, 101

Hampshire County Cricket Club, D-40 team 119, 124

Harley, Captain Mike 58, 63

Harrison, Corporal of Horse Craig, *The Longest Kill* 92-3

Harrison Point, St Lucy, Barbados 20

Hawkins, Nigel 44

Haynes, Alvin 34

Haynes, Frankie 7

Haynes, Jesse 123

Haynes, Lisa 22-3

Headley Court (Defence Medical Rehabilitation Centre DMRC) 110-14, 149

helicopters
  Apache 85, 89, 95
  Chinook 85, 96
  Merlin 91
  Angel Flights 96
  see also MERT

Helmand Province 83
  Forward Operating Base Edinburgh *x, xi,* 85
  Musa Qala *x,* 83, 87
  Horseshoe Ridge 94-5
  PB Habib 94-7
  PB Woqab 94

Help for Heroes (H4H) *xi,* 121, 127, 130
  funding for Para Bobsleigh 133, 136, 142
  High Performance Academy 142

Henson, Dave 127

Hilton, Ben 91

Holkham, Norfolk 55

Holliday, Corporal of Horse Paul 'Doc' 118

Horse Guards Parade, Whitehall, Queen's Life Guard 59, 61-2, 65-6, 67

Hothersal Primary School, Barbados 10-11

Household Cavalry 45, 149
  The Blues and Royals 45
  The Life Guards 45
  see also Household Cavalry Mounted Regiment (HCMR); Household Cavalry Regiment (HCR)

Household Cavalry Foundation (HCF) 120-1, 136, 142, 172

Household Cavalry Mounted Regiment (HCMR) 45, 51-67, 115
  'box men' duty 59, 66-7
  Khaki Ride training 51-5
    Egypt Ride 52, 53, 55
  Kit training 57-61
  Mounted Escorts 57, 61, 63, 65
  Life Guards' Mounted Squadron, 3 Troop 58
  state ceremonial and public duties 59-62, 65-6
  Watering Order 64

Household Cavalry Museum 62, 66

Household Cavalry Operational Casualties Fund 142

Household Cavalry Pageant (2007) 66

Household Cavalry Regiment (HCR) 45, 83
  A Squadron 68-70, 75, 78, 83
  C Squadron 79-80, 83, 85-7, 89, 91-5, 113-14
  3 Troop *xi,* 86
  return from Afghanistan 113
  Medals Parade 114
  RHQ 83, 87, 116

Household Division, Foot Guards 12, 36, 55, 66

Hunt, Sergeant Nathan 85

Hunte, Laura 169

Hurricane Ivan (2004), Grenada 37
Husbands, Sir Clifford, Governor
  General of Barbados 27
Hyde Park Barracks *see* Knightsbridge

Ian (prosthetics expert) 109, 111
IEDs (Improvised Explosive Devices)
  x, 84
  clearance teams 86
  encounters with 88–9
Igls, Austria, Para Bobsleigh 135–6
Igo, Gareth 44
Independence Day Parades, Barbados
  20, 21, 117
Indi Marketing, Bridgetown 20
International Bobsleigh and Skeleton
  Federation 132
International Security Assistance
  Force (ISAF) 83
Invictus Games
  (2014) 127, 128–31
  (2016) 131
  (2017) 131
Ireland, Staff Corporal 'Paddy' 85

Jelinek, Captain Andrew 106, 108
Joll, Christopher (co-author) 66, 142,
  156
Jordan, Andre 21
Julian, Bombardier Fayanne 44

Kate the Aussie 111–13
Kensington Oval, Bridgetown 17
Kibble, Captain Les 44, 45, 50, 51
Knightsbridge, Hyde Park Barracks 68
  Kit training 57–61
Kovac, Branislav 126

Kwik, Mike 134

Lakenheath, RAF 55
Lavrinc, Ziva 145–6
Leacock, Corporal Mike 49
Lewin, Surgeon Lieutenant Colonel
  Jedge 92, 93
LimbPower Games 119
Limbu, Kushal 127
Lipman, Damien 168
London Paralympic Games (2012) 119
Long, David 139–40, 144, 146
Lulworth Camp, Dorset, AFV
  Gunnery School 70

MacCauliffe, Aiden 50
Mcgeachy, Trooper Robbie 'Geach'
  100
McGeary, Sergeant 30, 35–6
McGuire, John 108
McGuire, Troop Corporal of Horse
  Matthew 'Jerry' *xii*, 79, 86, 90, 93
  and IEDs 88–9, 95, 97
  account of IED explosion 99–102, 108
  in Barbados 118
  support for CM 121
McMullen, Captain Sean 108, 109, 113
Mapp, Agnes 'Pinky' (mother) 5–6,
  7, 80
  and death of husband 34–5
  in London 60, 78
  at Passing Off parade 61
  to England 104–5
Mapp, Alexa 91, 103
  birth 78
Mapp, Andrew 6
Mapp, Burkley 6, 35

Mapp, Corie
  birth 3, 6-7
  childhood 3-10
  primary schools 10-11, 12, 13-16
  first visit to England 12
  sport
    cricket 13, 15, 17
    volleyball 21, 70-1
  secondary education 16-18
  groin injury 16, 46, 71, 78
  joins Cadets 16-17
  Barbados Youth Service 18, 19-20
  at polytechnic 20-1
  as Parish Ambassador 22-3
  Royal Barbados Police Force 23-7
    transfer to RRU 27-9
    move to Canine Unit 30-2, 35-6
    with SSU 36-40
    resignation from RBPF 40-1
  Royal Marines selection 33
  death of father 34-5
  signs up with British Army 41-2
  at Pirbright 42, 43-51
  joins The Life Guards 50-1
  posted to Household Cavalry
  Mounted Regiment (HCMR) 51-67
    Khaki Ride training, Egypt Ride 52
    Kit training 57-61
  family brought to London 56
  posted to Household Cavalry
  Regiment 68-70
    gunnery training 69-70
    training in Canada (BATUS) 71-5
    Regimental Quarter.'s stores 78, 79
    service extension 91
  deployment to Afghan. 80-1, 83-98
  financial problems 91, 107

Mapp, Corie, continued
  injured by IED xi-xii, 1, 97-8, 99-102
  hospitalised in Birmingham 1-2,
    103-9, 149
  recovery 105-9
  at Headley Court 110-14
  tailoring 115-16
  promotion to Corporal 116-17
  medical discharge from Brit. Army 121
  disabled sport
    cricket 112, 114, 119, 124
    golf 112, 114, 120, 124
    sitting volleyball 112, 114, 119-20,
      124-7, 129-31
    athletics 127, 130
    Para Bobsleigh 132-47
  land and house in Barbados 109, 114,
    122
  move to Swindon 123
  thoughts on policing and racism
    148-55
  continuing ambitions 149-51
Mapp, Erin 56, 62, 103, 104
  birth 30
  at school 60, 61
Mapp, Jacqueline 'Jackie' (Mrs Alvin
    Haynes) 2, 6, 7, 34
  at Birmingham 104-5, 107
  move to Swindon 123
Mapp, Jodie 49, 56, 103, 104
  birth 38
Mapp, Marie 'Sissy' (Mrs Wayne
    Mayers) 5, 6, 10-12, 34
  visits to England 12, 29, 41-2, 77
  to Birmingham 104-5
Mapp, Marketha 2, 34, 125
  first meeting 22

Mapp, Marketha, continued
  marriage 29–30
  children 30, 35, 77, 78
  in London 56, 60, 66
  at Passing Off parade 61
  married quarters in Windsor 68, 102,
    122–3
  and CM's deployment to
  Afghanistan 80–1
  and Christmas leave 91
  phone calls to 95, 97
  and news of CM's injuries 102–5
  return to Barbados 118–19, 122
  honeymoon in St Lucia 118
  move to Swindon 123
  job with NHS 123
Mapp, Merleen 'Joyce' 5, 6
Mapp, Monica 'Fay' (Mrs Frankie
  Haynes) 6, 7
Mapp, Rudolph (father) 5, 6, 8–9, 23, 25
  illness 8, 33–4
  and CM's marriage 30
  death 34–5
marijuana ('weed')
  illegal farm in Barbados 28
  huge stash 31
  passive find 31–2
Marineau, Dennis 141
Marley, Bob 153
Massiah Street, Barbados 6
Maycock, Station Sergeant 24
Mayers, Errol 'Wayne' 5, 12–13, 22,
  56, 104
Medicine Hat, Alberta, Canada 74–5
Menya, Sergeant Alex 119, 124
MERT (Medical Emergency Reponse
  Team), Afghanistan 96

MeToo movement 152
Miller, Mercedes 134–5
Minichiello, Nicola 137
Monk, Sarah 134, 136, 141
Mothers' Union, Barbados 7
Mott, Garrison Sergeant Major Billy 67
Mount Doom (Mount Musa Qala) 94–7
Mount Tabor Primary school,
  Barbados 15–16
Mowatt, Lance Corporal of Horse
  Donovan 44
Musa Qala, Helmand Province x, 83, 87
Forward Line of Enemy Troops
  (FLET) 87

Newell, Staff Corporal 'Nudger' 92
Nichols, Captain Ralston 16–17
Norris, Sergeant 44

Obeah woman, Barbados 4
O'Farrell, Clifford 'Cliff' 106, 108
Oistins Fish Festival, Barbados 38
Op BARMA, IED clearance teams 80, 86
Operation EAGLE, Barbados 27–8
Operation HERRICK 7, Afghanistan
  75, 83
Operation HERRICK 8, Afghanistan
  75, 83
Operation HERRICK 11, Afghanistan
  79, 83–98
Operation MINIMISE, repatriation of
  casualties from Afghanistan 84
Operation TELIC 10, Iraq 70

Padmore, Stephen 169
Para Bobsleigh 132–47
  Calgary 133–5, 141, 143, 144, 145

Para Bobsleigh, continued
  funding for 133, 136, 142–3
  Igls, Austria 135–6, 139
  World Cup 136–9, 143–4, 146, 147
  sleds 137, 138, 139, 143
  St Moritz 138–9, 145
  Lake Placid 140–1, 143, 144, 145–6
  Park City, Salt Lake City 141, 146
  Lillehammer 144, 145
  Oberhof 144, 145
  World Championships 144, 146–7
  European Championships 146
  La Plagne, France 147
  ambition to coach 150
Paradise Village, Barbados 31
Paralympic Day, sitting volleyball
  National Cup 125
Pax Military Insurance 107
Pettipher, Corp. of Horse Anthony 79
Phelan, Lance Corporal of Horse
  Andrew 70, 72, 73, 74, 75
Philipson-Stowe, Mrs 108
Phillip, Lieutenant Colonel Rhodri
  109, 120, 130
Phillips, Trevor 154
Porter, Trooper 'Dangerous' Dave 92, 93
Porter, Trooper Scott 'Scotty' 86, 87,
  93, 95, 113
  IED clearance 97
  and IED explosion 99, 100, 101–2
  in Selly Oak 106, 108
Prince, donkey 10

Queen Elizabeth Hospital,
  Bridgetown, Barbados 3, 34–5, 122
Queen Elizabeth Hospital, Selly Oak,
  Birmingham 1–2, 103–5, 105–9, 149

racial prejudice 63–4, 151–2
  need for education 152–3
RAF Brize Norton 84
Rastafarians 39
Read, Captain Dan 96
Read, PC Kay 40
REME (Royal Electrical and
  Mechanical Engineers), LAD 76, 93
Remembrance Day, Barbados 21
Reynolds, Bombardier Robby 44, 45, 50
Richardson, Matt 133, 137, 141
Riley, Joseph 19–20
Robertson, Rt Hon Sir Hugh, KCMG,
  DL *viii–ix*
Roosevelt, Franklin D., US President 150
Royal Anglian Regiment (Vikings), in
  Afghanistan 87, 94, 97, 100
Royal Artillery (RA), in Afghanistan 87
Royal Barbados Police Force 23–7, 117
  night-time patrols 21
  Regional Police Training Centre
    24–5
  Rapid Response Unit (RRU) 27–9
  Special Services Unit (SSU) 27–8, 29,
    36–40
  Canine Unit 30–2
  Commissioner's Parade 31
  Drug Squad 31, 36
Royal British Legion (RBL) 130
  campaign 142
Royal Engineers (RE), Brimstone mine
  clearance teams 86
Royal Marines, Commando Training
  Centre, Lympstone 33
Ryan, Kath (the Cake Lady) 108

Saint John parish, Barbados 4-5, 22-3
    CM as Parish Ambassador 22-3
Saint John's Cultural Cricket Club 13
Saint John's Parish Church, Barbados
    7, 30, 35
Samuel Jackman Prescod Polytechnic,
    Saint Michael 20-1
Samuel, Tom 143
Sanford Prince, racehorse 8
Seacole, Mary 154
Seale, Sir David 8
Sealy, Graydon 22
Selly Oak hospital *see* Queen
    Elizabeth Hospital
slave trade, views of 154
Slavery Abolition Act (1833) 3
Smith, Dwayne 17
social media 153
Spence, Sir Basil 57
Spooner, Sergeant 37, 38-9
Stanford, Christine 25
State ceremonial
    Queen's Life Guard on Whitehall 59,
        61-2
    State Opening of Parliament 59, 65
    Queen's Birthday Parade (Trooping
        the Colour) 65
    State Visits 65-6
Stephens, Station Sergeant Dale 25
Stewart, Miss 15
Stonewall 152
Storer, Pete 168
Stores, Corporal 'Ads' 93
Stuart, John 21
Sturm, Jason 136-7, 139, 140, 141, 145-6
Swindon, house in 123

Taliban *x*, 83
    operation to clear from Helmand
        91-7
    'dickers' (target spotters) 92-3, 94, 97
Thistlethwaite, Kelly 111-12, 113
Thompson, Terry 27-8, 50
    Royal Marines selection 33
Toby, Corporal of Horse 53
Trail's End Camp, Canada 75
Trodden, Ashley 119
Trooping the Colour (Queen's
    Birthday Parade) 65
Twumasi-Ankrah, Captain Nana 'TA'
    44, 45-6, 49-50, 51, 58

Uganda 124
United Kingdom 153
United States, race in 153
US Army, in Afghanistan 84

Vallon metal detector 80, 84, 87
vehicles
    Spartan armoured personnel carrier 72
    Challenger tank 74
    Salamander light tank 76
    Mastiff armoured patrol vehicle
        78-9, 85
    Scimitar CVR(T) 89-90, 93

Waincott, Trooper 63
Wales, Captain Harry (aka HRH
    Prince Henry of Wales, Duke of
    Sussex) 53
    in Canada 75-7
    and Invictus Games 128, 130, 131
Walker, Charlie 126

Walker, Station Sergeant 37-8

Ward, Richard 90-1, 106

Warrington, Susan 14

Warrior Games 129
  Colorado Springs 125, 126-7

Watson, Louise 133, 135

Waygood, Major Dicky, Riding
  Master 53, 136

Webb, Matt 127

Went, Peter 21

Williams, Trooper Oliver 'Oli' 80, 81, 86

Wiltshire, Miss 15

Wiltshire Police, new career with 150, 156

Windrush scandal 155

Winter Olympics, Sochi (2014) 120, 136

Wootton Bassett (now Royal Wootton
  Bassett) *xi*, 84

Woqab, Helmand, Patrol Base (PB) 94

Worrell, PC Gladstone 37, 39

Yankee, Life Guards 'black' 60

Yorkshire Regiment, in Afghanistan 87

Young, Claudine (grandmother)
  10-11, 16

Young, Fitz (uncle) 12, 33, 41, 43

Young, Herbert 14

Young, Michelle 13-14

Ypres, Belgium, Menin Gate 49

Zeus, Life Guards 'black' 63

ACKNOWLEDGEMENTS

The authors would like to thank Les Ferdinand MBE and Sir Hugh Robertson KCMG PC DL for their contributions, respectively, of a Preface and a Foreword; and Barney Campbell for 'A Personal View', and the photographs of the Household Cavalry Regiment on operational deployment in Afghanistan. They would also like to thank former Staff Corporal Matthew 'Jerry' McGuire and Marketha Mapp for recalling painful memories of the events of 31st January 2010 and afterwards.

This book would not have happened if former Life Guards officer, Damien Lipman, had not proposed that it be written and then e-introduced the authors. Other Household Cavalrymen who helped in the writing of this story include Lieutenant Colonel Ralph Griffin (Regimental Adjutant, Household Cavalry); Colonel Harry Fullerton OBE (Corie Mapp's Commanding Officer in Afghanistan); Pete Storer (Curator, Household Cavalry Museum); and Samantha Wyndham, whose forebears have served as Life Guards since 1660 and who edited the book *pro bono*.

Other people whose contributions are here acknowledged and thanked include Major (now Lieutenant Colonel) Stuart Milsom-Smith, Company Commander of 'A' Company, 1 Royal Anglian Regiment (The Vikings) in 2010 for his photographs of Corie's wrecked CVR(T); the internationally renowned equine and military photographer Henry Dallal, for the cover image of Corie for which he refused to accept a fee; and, of course, Anthony Weldon, formerly of the Irish Guards, who is the book's publisher.

Although their contributions are detailed in the text, Corie Mapp would like to record here his particular thanks to the Medical Emergency Response Team and the staff at the military hospital at Camp Bastion, Afghanistan, who saved his life; all the staff of the Queen Elizabeth Hospital (formerly Selly Oak), Birmingham, and the Defence Medical Rehabilitation Centre, Headley Court, who put him back on his feet; former Blues and Royals officer, Rupert Fryer, Help for Heroes, Blesma, the Royal British Legion, and the Household Cavalry Foundation for their financial support, which has enabled him to achieve sporting success; and Anna Greco, David Long, Renier Grace and Lonnie Bissonnette for their total belief in him, even at times when he didn't believe in himself. In addition to those mentioned above, Corie would also like to thank Stephen Padmore and Laura Hunte, whose names do not appear in the text, but who in various different ways have contributed to his life and his success. Finally, Corie thanks from the bottom of his heart his wife, daughters and family for their unfailing love, without which there would have been no story to tell.

ABOUT THE CO-AUTHOR

After the Royal Military Academy Sandhurst and Oxford University, Christopher Joll spent his formative years as an officer in The Life Guards. On leaving the Army, Joll worked first in investment banking, but the boredom of City life led him to switch careers and become an arms sales-man. After ten years of dealing with tin pot dictators in faraway countries, he moved – perhaps appropriately – into public relations where, in this new incarnation, he had to deal with dictators of an altogether different type.

From his earliest days, Joll has written articles, features, short stories and reportage. He is the author of *Uniquely British: A Year in the Life of the Household Cavalry* (Tricorn Books), *The Drum Horse in the Fountain: Tales of the Heroes & Rogues in the Guards* (Nine Elms Books), *Spoils of War: The Treasures, Trophies & Trivia of the British Empire* (Nine Elms Books), *The Imperial Impresario: The Treasures, Trophies & Trivia of Napoleon's Theatre of Power* (Nine Elms Books), and numerous articles for national and regimental periodicals. He is also the author of the nine-volume historical action-adventure series *The Speedicut Papers* and the follow-on six volume series *The Speedicut Memoirs*, the concluding volume of which was published in 2020. He has recently completed his yet to be published memoires, *Anecdotal Evidence*, and is currently working on a book about Madame Tussaud's Napoléonica, lost in a fire in 1925, and planning a second book with Corie Mapp.

Since leaving the Army, Joll has also been involved in devising, scripting, directing and (occasionally) producing charity fund-raising events. These include the Household Cavalry Pageant (2007), the Chelsea Pageant (2008), the Diamond Jubilee Parade in the Park (2012), the British Military Tournament (2010-2013), the Gurkha Bicentenary Pageant (2015), the Waterloo Bicentenary National Service of Commemoration & Parade at St Paul's Cathedral (2015), the Shakespeare 400 Memorial Concert (2016), The Patron's Lunch (the official London event in 2016) to mark The Queen's 90th Birthday, and the royal premiere of *The Great War Symphony* at the Royal Albert Hall (2018), for which he researched and directed an hour-long backing video using Imperial War Museum archive footage.

When not writing, or directing 'military theatre', Joll is a lecturer for Viking Cruises and Noble Caledonia, provides military/historical research to auctioneers Sworders and Cheffins, speaks at literary and history festivals around the UK, is a video podcaster on the YouTube channel, and is a Trustee of The Art Fund Prize for Museums.   *www.christopherjoll.com*

ABOUT THE HOUSEHOLD CAVALRY FOUNDATION

The Household Cavalry Foundation (HCF) is the official charity for the Household Cavalry. It provides charitable and pastoral support to all the members of the Household Cavalry 'family': our serving soldiers, operational casualties, veterans and dependants. The Foundation also supports the Household Cavalry's heritage, and the welfare of our retired horses.

Since the Restoration of the Monarchy in 1660, the four antecedent Regiments of today's Household Cavalry (The 1st and 2nd Life Guards, the Royal Horse Guards (The Blues), and the 1st (Royal) Dragoons), and their modern successors in The Life Guards and The Blues and Royals, have fought in every major British Army campaign, most recently in the Falkland Islands, Iraq and Afghanistan, and have been deployed on peace-keeping duty in Ulster, Cyprus, the Balkans and Eastern Europe. As a result of these, and anticipating future conflicts, the HCF cares for physical injuries, and also prepares for long-term psychological problems, such as Post-Traumatic Stress Disorder (PTSD), that tend to emerge long after operational tours.

The Household Cavalry Foundation relies solely on public donations. For more information about the HCF, please visit *www.hcavfoundation.org*, email *director@hcavfoundation.org*, or call +44(0) 20 7 839 4858.

Charity Commission Number 1151869. Company Number 08236363

Nine Elms is an independent specialist
imprint that is dedicated to bringing you
the most creative and interesting minds
in contemporary writing today.

From crime fiction and history to biography,
Nine Elms features a diverse list of titles,
showcasing both well established and
exciting new authors.

* * *

NINE ELMS BOOKS
Unit 6B, Clapham North Arts Centre,
26-32 Voltaire Road, London SW4 6DH

TEL +44 (0)20 7720 6767
EMAIL info@nineelmsbooks.co.uk
WEB nineelmsbooks.co.uk

*

The
DRUM HORSE
in the FOUNTAIN

& Other Tales of Heroes and Rogues in the Guards

CHRISTOPHER JOLL & ANTHONY WELDON

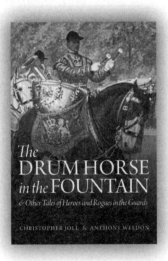

'To dip in and out of this book is immensely enjoyable.'

The Daily Telegraph

Co-authors Christopher Joll and Anthony Weldon capture the careers, accomplishments, follies and the occasional crimes of over three hundred of the officers and men, many of whom have been forgotten or overlooked, who, since King Charles II, have served in the seven Regiments of the Guards.

They have earned forty-four Victoria Crosses, founded the SAS, led the WW2 development of the Commandos and acted as spies, double agents and spy masters. Also included are extraordinary cast of characters such as the preferred candidate for the throne of Albani, one UK and two N Ireland Prime Ministers, plus a whole host of Cabinet Ministers, and an Archbishop of Canterbury, known as 'Killer', with an MC.

In other spheres, there have been championship boxers, footballers and Olympic medallists; best-selling authors, playwrights and composers; singing sensations, international musicians in the fields of pop, jazz, light and classical music as well as comedians, artists, and two Oscar-winning film stars.

Hbk | 234 × 156 mm | 314 pages | ISBN 978-1-910533-40-6 £20.00   Ebk | ISBN 978-1-910533-41-3 £4.99

www.nineelmsbooks.co.uk

SPOILS OF WAR

by CHRISTOPHER JOLL

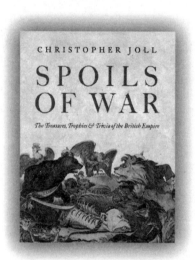

'Each of these trophies of victory, ranging from the priceless to the valueless, has a story which Joll recounts – and sometimes debunks – with style, humour and insight'

Michael Portillo

Over the last seven hundred years the United Kingdom has acquired a staggering array of treasures as a direct result of its military activities – from Joan of Arc's ring to the Rock of Gibraltar to Hitler's desk. *Spoils of War* describes these spoils and how they came to be acquired as well as telling the tales of some of the extraordinary (and extraordinarily incompetent) men and women, now mostly forgotten, who had a hand in the rise and fall of the British Empire. Along the way the book debunks a significant number of myths, exposes a major fraud perpetrated on a leading London museum, reveals previously unknown spoils of war and casts light on some very dark corners of Britain's military history

'Christopher Joll has a magpie's eye for a story, combined with the dogged research skills to sniff out and solve mysteries. No one is better equipped to ignite history in this tangible and novel way.'

Philip Mould, presenter, *Antiques Roadshow* and *Fake or Fortune?*

Hardback | 246 × 189 mm | 320 pages | Illustrated throughout | ISBN 978-1-910533-46-8 £25.00

www.nineelmsbooks.co.uk